The Defining Decade

The Defining Decade

Why Your **Twenties** Matter and How to Make the Most of Them **Now**

MEG JAY, PhD

TWELVE

NEW YORK BOSTON

The advice herein is not intended to replace the services of trained mental health professionals. You are advised to consult with your health care professional with regard to matters relating to your mental health, and in particular regarding matters that may require diagnosis or medical attention. The author and publisher specifically disclaim any liability that is incurred from the use or application of the contents of this book.

Twelve
Hachette Book Group
237 Park Avenue
New York, NY 10017

www.HachetteBookGroup.com

Printed in the United States of America
RRD-C

First Edition: April 2012

Twelve is an imprint of Grand Central Publishing.
The Twelve name and logo are trademarks of Hachette Book Group, Inc.

10 9 8 7 6 5

Library of Congress Cataloging-in-Publication Data

Jay, Meg.
The defining decade : why your twenties matter and how to make the most of them now / Meg Jay. — 1st ed.
p. cm.
ISBN 978-0-446-56176-1
1. Adulthood. I. Title.
BF724.5 .J39
115.6'5—dc23

2011044830

For Jay and Hazel

AUTHOR'S NOTE

This book is about my work with twentysomethings, as a clinical psychologist in private practice in Charlottesville, Virginia, and as a clinical professor at the University of Virginia, and previously as a clinician in Berkeley, California, and a lecturer at University of California, Berkeley. Throughout these pages, I do my best to tell the personal, and sometimes poignant, stories of the clients and students who taught me about the twentysomething years. To protect their privacy, I have changed their names and the details of their lives. In many cases, I have created composites from those with similar experiences and with whom I had similar sessions and conversations. I hope every twentysomething who reads this book sees him- or herself in the stories I include, but a resemblance to any particular twentysomething is coincidental.

CONTENTS

Contents

PREFACE

The Defining Decade

In a rare study of life-span development, researchers at Boston University and University of Michigan examined dozens of life stories, written by prominent, successful people toward the end of their lives. They were interested in "autobiographically consequential experiences," or the circumstances and people that had the strongest influence on how life unfolded thereafter. While important events took place from birth until death, those that determined the years ahead were most heavily concentrated during the twenty-something years.

It would make sense that as we leave home or college and become more independent there is a burst of self-creation, a time when what we do determines who we will become. It might even seem like adulthood is one long stretch of autobiographically consequential experiences—that the older we get, the more we direct our own lives. This is not true.

In our thirties, consequential experiences start to slow. School will be over or nearly so. We will have invested time in careers or made the choice not to. We, or our friends, may be in relationships and starting families. We may own homes or have other responsibilities that make it difficult to change directions. With about 80 percent of life's most significant events taking place by age thirty-five, as thirtysomethings and beyond we largely either continue with, or correct for, the moves we made during our twentysomething years.

The deceptive irony is that our twentysomething years may not feel all that consequential. It is easy to imagine that life's significant experiences begin with big moments and exciting encounters, but this is not how it happens.

Researchers in this same study found that most of the substantial and lasting events—those that led to career success, family fortune, personal bliss, or lack thereof—developed across days or weeks or months with little immediate dramatic effect. The importance of these experiences was not necessarily clear at the time but, in retrospect, the subjects recognized that these events had sharply defined their futures. To a great extent, our lives are decided by far-reaching twentysomething moments we may not realize are happening at all.

This book is about recognizing those defining twentysomething moments. It's about why your twenties matter, and how to make the most of them now.

INTRODUCTION

Real Time

Tired of lying in the sunshine, staying home to watch the rain
You are young and life is long, and there is time to kill today
And then one day you find, ten years has got behind you
No one told you when to run, you missed the starting gun.

—David Gilmour, Nick Mason, Roger Waters, and Richard Wright of Pink Floyd, "Time"

Almost invariably, growth and development has what's called a critical period. There's a particular period of maturation in which, with external stimulation of the appropriate kind, the capacity will pretty suddenly develop and mature. Before that and later than that, it's either harder or impossible.

—Noam Chomsky, linguist

When Kate started therapy, she had been waiting tables and living—and fighting—with her parents for more than a year. Her father called to schedule her first appointment, and both of them presumed that father-daughter issues would come quickly to the fore. But what most struck me about Kate was that her twentysomething years were wasting away. Having grown up in New York City, at age twenty-six and now living in Virginia, she still did not have a driver's license, despite the fact that this limited her employment opportunities and made her feel like a passenger in her own life. Not unrelated to this, Kate was often late to our appointments.

When Kate graduated from college, she had hoped to experience the expansiveness of the twentysomething years, something she was strongly encouraged to do by her parents. Her mother and father married just out of college because they wanted to go to Europe together and, in the early 1970s, this was not condoned by either of their families. They honeymooned in Italy and came back pregnant. Kate's dad put his accounting degree to work while Kate's mom got busy raising four kids, of whom Kate was the youngest. So far, Kate had spent her own twenties trying to make up for what her parents missed. She thought she was supposed to be having the time of her life but mostly she felt stressed and anxious. "My twenties are paralyzing," she said. "No one told me it would be this hard."

Kate filled her mind with twentysomething drama to distract herself from the real state of her life, and she seemed to want the same for her therapy hours. When she came to sessions, she kicked off her Toms, hiked up her jeans, and caught me up on the weekend. Our conversations often went multimedia as she pulled up e-mails and photos to show me, and texts chirped into our sessions with late-breaking news.

Somewhere between the weekend updates, I found out the following: She thought she might like to work in fund-raising, and she hoped to figure out what she wanted to do by age thirty. "Thirty is the new twenty," she said. This was my cue.

I am too passionate about the twenties to let Kate, or any other twentysomething, waste his or her time. As a clinical psychologist who specializes in adult development, I have seen countless twentysomethings spend too many years living without perspective. What is worse are the tears shed by thirtysomethings and fortysomethings because they are now paying a steep price—professionally, romantically, economically, reproductively—for a lack of vision in their twenties. I liked Kate and wanted to help her so I insisted she be on time for sessions. I interrupted stories about the latest hookup to ask about the status of her driver's license and her job search. Perhaps most important, Kate and I debated about what therapy—and her twenties—was supposed to be about.

Kate wondered aloud whether she ought to spend a few years in therapy figuring out her relationship with her father or whether she should use that money and time on a Eurail pass to search for who she was. I voted for neither. I told Kate that while most therapists would agree with Socrates that "the unexamined life is not worth living," a lesser-known quote by American psychologist Sheldon Kopp might be more important here: "The unlived life is not worth examining."

I explained it would be irresponsible of me to sit quietly while I watched the most foundational years of Kate's life go parading by. It would be reckless for us to focus on Kate's past when I knew her future was in danger. It seemed unfair to talk about her weekends when it was her weekdays that made her so unhappy. I also genuinely felt that Kate's relationship with her father could not change until she had something new to bring to it.

Not long after these conversations, Kate dropped onto the couch in my office. Uncharacteristically teary and agitated, she stared out the window and bounced her legs nervously as she told me about Sunday brunch with four friends from college. Two were in town for a conference. One had just returned from recording lullabies in Greece for her dissertation research. Another brought along her fiancé. As the group sat at their table, Kate looked around and felt behind. She wanted what her friends had—a job or a purpose or a boyfriend—so she spent the rest of the day looking for leads on Craigslist. Most of the jobs (and the men) didn't seem interesting. The ones that did she was starting to doubt she could get. Kate went to bed feeling vaguely betrayed.

In my office, she said, "My twenties are more than half over. Sitting at that restaurant, I realized I didn't have anything to show for myself. No real résumé. No relationship. I don't even know what I'm doing in this town." She reached for a tissue and broke into tears. "I really got kicked by the notion that getting clear on your path was overrated. I wish I'd been more... I don't know... *intentional*."

It wasn't too late for Kate, but she did need to get going. By the time Kate's therapy ended, she had her own apartment, a driver's license, a boyfriend with some potential, and a job as a fund-raiser for a nonprofit. Even her relationship with her father was improving. In our last sessions together,

Kate thanked me for helping her catch up. She said she finally felt like she was living her life "in real time."

The twentysomething years *are* real time and ought to be lived that way. A thirty-is-the-new-twenty culture has told us that the twenties don't matter. Freud once said, "Love and work, work and love... that's all there is," and these things take shape later than they used to.

When Kate's parents were in their twenties, the average twenty-one-year-old was married and caring for a new baby. School ended with high school or maybe college, and young parents focused on making money and keeping house. Because one income was typically enough to support a family, men worked but two-thirds of women did not. The men and women who did work could expect to stay in the same field for life. In those days, the median home price in the United States was $17,000. Divorce and the Pill were just becoming mainstream.

Then, in the span of one generation, came an enormous cultural shift. User-friendly birth control flooded the market and women flooded the workplace. By the new millennium, only about half of twentysomethings were married by age thirty and even fewer had children, making the twenties a time of newfound freedom. We began to hear that maybe college was too expensive and less necessary, yet graduate school was more necessary, and in either case there was time for "time off."

For hundreds of years, twentysomethings moved directly from being sons and daughters to being husbands and wives, but within just a few decades a new developmental period opened up. Waking up every day somewhere between their childhood homes and their own mortgages, twentysomethings like Kate weren't sure what to make of the time.

Almost by definition, the twenties became a betwixt-and-between time. A 2001 article in the *Economist* introduced the "Bridget Jones Economy" and a 2005 cover of *Time* ran with a headline "Meet the Twixters," both of which informed us that the twenties were now disposable years lubricated by disposable income. By 2007, the twenties were dubbed the odyssey years, a time meant for wandering. And journalists and researchers everywhere began to refer to twentysomethings with silly nicknames such as kidults, pre-adults, and adultescents.

Some say the twentysomething years are an extended adolescence while others call them an emerging adulthood. This so-called changing timetable for adulthood has demoted twentysomethings to "not-quite-adults" just when they need to engage the most. Twentysomethings like Kate have been caught in a swirl of hype and misunderstanding, much of which has trivialized what is actually the most defining decade of our adult lives.

Yet even as we dismiss the twentysomething years, we fetishize them. The twentysomething years have never been more in the zeitgeist. Popular culture has an almost obsessive focus on the twenties such that these freebie years appear to be all that exist. Child celebrities and everyday kids spend their youth acting twenty, while mature adults and the Real Housewives dress, and are sculpted, to look twenty-nine. The young look older and the old look younger, collapsing the adult lifespan into one long twentysomething ride. Even a new term—amortality—has been coined to describe living the same way, at the same pitch, from our teens until death.

This is a contradictory and dangerous message. We are led to believe the twentysomething years don't matter, yet, with the glamorization of and near obsession with the twenties, there is little to remind us that anything else ever will. This causes too many men and women to squander the most transformative years of their adult lives, only to pay the price in decades to come.

Our cultural attitude toward the twenties is something like good old American irrational exuberance. Twenty-first-century twentysomethings have grown up alongside the dot-com craze, the supersize years, the housing bubble, and the Wall Street boom. Start-ups imagined slick websites would generate money and demand; individuals failed to consider the fat and calories that went along with supersizing fast food; homeowners banked on ever-appreciating homes; financial managers envisioned markets always on the rise. Adults of all ages let what psychologists call "unrealistic optimism"—the idea that nothing bad will ever happen to you—overtake logic and reason. Adults of all backgrounds failed to do the math. Now twentysomethings have been set up to be another bubble ready to burst.

Inside my office, I have seen the bust.

The Great Recession and its continuing aftermath have left many twentysomethings feeling naïve, even devastated. Twentysomethings are more educated than ever before, but a smaller percentage find work after college. Many entry-level jobs have gone overseas making it more difficult for twentysomethings to gain a foothold at home. With a contracting economy and a growing population, unemployment is at its highest in decades. An unpaid internship is the new starter job. About a quarter of twentysomethings are out of work and another quarter work only part-time. Twentysomethings who do have paying jobs earn less than their 1970s counterparts when adjusted for inflation.

Because short-term work has replaced long-term careers in our country, as jobs come and go so do twentysomethings themselves. The average twentysomething will have more than a handful of jobs in their twenties alone. One-third will move in any given year, leaving family and friends and résumés and selves scattered. About one in eight go back home to live with Mom or Dad, at least in part because salaries are down and college debt is up, with the number of students owing more than $40,000 having increased tenfold in the past ten years.

It seems everybody wants to be a twentysomething except for many twentysomethings themselves. All around, "thirty is the new twenty" is starting to get a new reaction: "God, I hope not."

Every day, I work with twentysomethings who feel horribly deceived by the idea that their twenties would be the best years of their lives. People imagine that to do therapy with twentysomethings is to listen to the adventures and misadventures of carefree people, and there is some of that. But behind closed doors, my clients have unsettling things to say:

- I feel like I'm in the middle of the ocean. Like I could swim in any direction but I can't see land on any side so I don't know which way to go.

- I feel like I just have to keep hooking up and see what sticks.
- I didn't know I'd be crying in the bathroom at work every day.
- The twentysomething years are a whole new way of thinking about time. There's this big chunk of time and a whole bunch of stuff needs to happen somehow.
- My sister is thirty-five and single. I'm terrified that's going to happen to me.
- I can't wait to be liberated from my twenties.
- I'd better not still be doing this at thirty.
- Last night I prayed for just one thing in my life to be certain.

There are fifty million twentysomethings in the United States, most of whom are living with a staggering, unprecedented amount of uncertainty. Many have no idea what they will be doing, where they will be living, or who they will be with in two or even ten years. They don't know when they will be happy or when they will be able to pay their bills. They wonder if they should be photographers or lawyers or designers or bankers. They don't know whether they are a few dates or many years from a meaningful relationship. They worry about whether they will have families and whether their marriages will last. Most simply, they don't know if their lives will work out and they don't know what to do.

Uncertainty makes people anxious, and distraction is the twenty-first-century opiate of the masses. So twentysomethings like Kate are tempted, and even encouraged, to turn away and be twixters, to close their eyes and hope for the best. A 2011 article in *New York* magazine arguing that "the kids are actually sort of alright" explained that while today's twentysomethings face some of the worst economic conditions since World War II, they are optimistic. The article explained that with free music online "you don't need to have money to buy a huge record collection." Facebook, Twitter, Google, and free apps "have made life on a small budget a lot more diverting," it reassures.

There is a saying that "hope is a good breakfast but a bad supper." While hopefulness is a useful state of mind that may help many downtrodden twentysomethings get out of bed in the morning, at the end of the day they need more than optimism because at the end of their twenties many will want more than diversions and record collections.

I know this because even more compelling than my sessions with struggling twentysomethings are my sessions with the earliest twixters, the now-thirtysomethings and forty-somethings who wish they had done some things differently. I have witnessed the true heartache that accompanies the realization that life is not going to add up. We may hear that thirty is the new twenty, but—recession or not—when it comes to work and love and the brain and the body, forty is definitely not the new thirty.

Many twentysomethings assume life will come together quickly after thirty, and maybe it will. But it is still going to be a different life. We imagine that if nothing happens in our twenties then everything is still possible in our thirties. We think that by avoiding decisions now, we keep all of our options open for later—but not making choices is a choice all the same.

When a lot has been left to do, there is enormous thirtysomething pressure to get ahead, get married, pick a city, make money, buy a house, enjoy life, go to graduate school, start a business, get a promotion, save for college and retirement, and have two or three children in a much shorter period of time. Many of these things are incompatible and, as research is just starting to show, simply harder to do all at the same time in our thirties.

Life does not end at thirty, but it does have a categorically different feel. A spotty résumé that used to reflect twentysomething freedom suddenly seems suspect and embarrassing. A good first date leads not so much to romantic fantasies about "The One" as to calculations about the soonest possible time marriage and a baby might happen.

Of course, for many it does happen and, upon the birth of their first child, thirtysomething couples often speak of new purpose and meaning. There can also be a deep and heart-wrenching sense of regret: knowing it will be difficult to provide for their child as they now wish they could; finding that fertility problems or sheer exhaustion stand in the way of the families they now want; realizing they will be nearly sixty when their children go to college and maybe seventy at their weddings; recognizing they may never know their own grandchildren.

Parents like Kate's are so intent on protecting their kids from *their* brand of the midlife crisis—*their* regret over settling down too soon—that these parents fail to see an entirely new midlife crisis is afoot. The postmillennial midlife crisis is figuring out that while we were busy making sure we didn't miss out on anything, we were setting ourselves up to miss out on some of the most important things of all. It is realizing that doing something later is not automatically the same as doing something better. Too many smart, well-meaning thirtysomethings and fortysomethings grieve a little as they face a lifetime of catching up. They look at themselves—and at me sitting across the room—and say about their twenties, "What was I *doing*? What was I *thinking*?"

I urge twentysomethings to reclaim their twenties, their status as adults, and their futures. This book will show them why they should and how they can.

In the pages ahead, I want to convince you that thirty is *not* the new twenty. Not because twentysomethings don't or shouldn't settle down later than their parents did. Most everyone agrees that work and love are happening later at least as much because of economics as because they can. I want to persuade you that thirty is not the new twenty precisely *because* we settle down later than we used to. What this has done is made the twenties not an irrelevant downtime but a developmental sweet spot that comes only once.

In almost all areas of development, there is what is called a critical period, a time when we are primed for growth and change, when simple exposure can lead to dramatic transformation. Children effortlessly learn whatever language they hear before the age of five. We develop binocular vision between three and eight months of age. These critical periods are windows of opportunity when learning happens quickly. Afterward, things are not so easy.

The twenties are that critical period of adulthood.

These are the years when it will be easiest to start the lives we want. And no matter what we do, the twenties are an inflection point—the great reorganization—a time when the experiences we have disproportionately influence the adult lives we will lead.

In sections titled "Work," "Love," and "The Brain and the Body," we will learn about four separate—but interwoven—critical periods that unfold across the twentysomething years. In "Work," we find out why twentysomething jobs are likely the most professionally and economically consequential we will ever have—even though they may not look so good. In "Love," we will hear why our twentysomething relationship choices may be even more important than those at work. And in "The Brain and the Body," we will learn how our still-developing twentysomething brains are wiring us to be the adults we will become just as our twentysomething bodies kick off our most fertile years.

Journalists may throw their hands up with headlines that read "What Is It About Twentysomethings?" and "Why Won't They Just Grow Up?," but the twenties aren't a mystery. We do know how the twenties work, and twentysomethings everywhere deserve to know it too.

In the chapters ahead, I blend the latest research on adult development with the previously untold stories of my clients and students. I will share what psychologists, sociologists, neurologists, economists, human resources executives, and reproductive specialists know about the unique power of the twentysomething years and how they shape our lives. Along the way, I challenge some media-driven misconceptions about the twenties, and show how common wisdom about the twentysomething years is often wrong.

We will find out why it's the people we hardly know, and not our closest friends, who will improve our lives most dramatically. We will learn how joining the world of work makes us feel better, not worse. We will hear why living together may not be the best way to test a relationship. We will learn how our personalities change more during our twenties than at any time before or after. We will see how we *do* pick our families, and not just our friends. We will understand how confidence grows not from the inside out, but from the outside in. We will hear how the stories we tell about ourselves affect whom we date and what jobs we get. We will start with why "Who am I?" is a question best answered not with a protracted identity crisis, but with one or two good pieces of something called identity capital.

Not long ago, twentysomethings like Kate's parents walked down the aisle before they thought through who they were. They made life's biggest decisions before their brains knew how to make them. Now twenty-first-century twentysomethings have the opportunity to build the lives they want—ones in which work, love, the brain and the body might all be in on it together. But this doesn't just happen with age, or optimism. It takes, as Kate said, intentionality, and some good information, or we will miss it. And for too long, good information has been hard to find.

A colleague of mine likes to say that twentysomethings are like airplanes, planes just leaving New York City bound for somewhere west. Right after takeoff, a slight change in course is the difference between landing in either Seattle or San Diego. But once a plane is nearly in San Diego, only a big detour will redirect it to the northwest.

Likewise, in the twentysomething years, even a small shift can radically change where we end up in our thirties and beyond. The twenties are an up-in-the-air and turbulent time, but if we can figure out how to navigate, even a little bit at a time, we can get further, faster, than at any other stage in life. It is a pivotal time when the things we do—and the things we don't do—will have an enormous effect across years and even generations to come.

So let's get going. The time is now.

WORK

Identity Capital

Adults don't emerge. They're made.
—Kay Hymowitz, social commentator

We are born not all at once, but by bits.
—Mary Antin, writer

Helen came to therapy because she was "having an identity crisis." She moved from nanny job to yoga retreat and back again as she waited for what she called "that lightning bolt of intuition." Helen always seemed dressed for an exercise class whether she was going to one or not and, for a time, her casual lifestyle was the envy of friends who had gone straight to the "real world," or its runner-up, graduate school. She came, she went. She enjoyed life for a while.

But before long, Helen's inner search for self became torturous. At twenty-seven, she felt as though the very friends who used to covet her adventures now pitied her. They were moving forward while she was pushing other people's babies around town in strollers.

Helen's parents had been specific about what college should be about: Tri-Delt and pre-med. All this despite the fact that Helen was a talented photographer who not-so-secretly wanted to major in art—and was not at all the sorority type. From her first semester, Helen hated pre-med classes and did poorly in them. She envied the interesting reading her friends were doing and grabbed every opportunity for artsy extracurriculars. After two years of suffering through biology requirements and packing her spare time with what she really enjoyed, Helen changed her major to art. Her parents said, "What are you going to do with *that*?"

After graduation, Helen tried her hand at freelance photography. Once the unpredictability of work began to affect her ability to pay her cell-phone bill, the life of an artist lost its luster. Without a pre-med degree, a clear future as a photographer, or even decent grades from college, Helen saw no way to move ahead. She wanted to stay in photography but wasn't sure how. She started nannying, the checks flowed under the table, the years ticked by, and her parents said, "We told you so."

Now Helen hoped that the right retreat or the right conversation in therapy or with friends might reveal, once and for all, who she was. Then, she said, she could get started on a life. I told her I wasn't so sure, and that an extended period of navel-gazing is usually counterproductive for twentysomethings.

"But this is what I'm supposed to be doing," Helen said.

"What is?" I asked.

"Having my crisis," she replied.

"Says who?" I asked.

"I don't know. Everybody. Books."

"I think you're misunderstanding what an identity crisis is and how you move out of one," I said. "Have you ever heard of Erik Erikson?"

Erik Salomonsen was a blond-haired German boy, born to a dark-haired mother and to a father he never knew. On Erik's third birthday, his mother married a local pediatrician who adopted Erik, making him Erik Homburger. They raised him in the Jewish tradition. At temple, Erik was teased for his fair complexion. At school, he was teased for being Jewish. Erik often felt confused about who he was.

After high school, Erik hoped to become an artist. He traveled around Europe, taking art classes and sometimes sleeping under bridges. At twenty-five, he returned to Germany and worked as an art teacher, studied Montessori education, got married, and started a family. After teaching the children of some very prominent psychoanalysts, Erik was analyzed by Sigmund Freud's daughter Anna, and he went on to earn a degree in psychoanalysis.

In his thirties, Erik moved his family to the United States, where he became a famed psychoanalyst and developmental theorist. He taught at Harvard, Yale, and Berkeley and wrote several books before winning a Pulitzer Prize. Hinting at his feelings of fatherlessness and his status as a self-made man, he changed his name to Erik Erikson, meaning "Erik, son of himself." Erik Erikson is best known for coining the term "identity crisis." It was 1950.

Despite being a product of the twentieth century, Erikson lived the life of a twenty-first-century man. He grew up in a blended family. He faced questions of cultural identity. He spent his teens and twenties in search of himself. At a time when adult roles were as ready-made as TV dinners, Erikson's experiences allowed him to imagine that an identity crisis was the norm, or at least ought to be. He felt that a true and authentic identity should not be rushed and, to that end, he advocated for a period of delay when youth could safely explore without real risk or obligation. For some, this period was college. For others, such as Erikson, it was a personal walkabout or *Wanderschaft*. Either way, he stressed the importance of coming into one's own. Erikson thought everyone should create his or her own life.

Helen and I talked about how Erikson went from identity crisis to the Pulitzer Prize. Yes, he traveled around and slept under some bridges. That's half the story. What else did he do? At twenty-five, he taught art and took some education classes. At twenty-six, he started training in psychoanalysis and met some influential people. By thirty, he'd earned his psychoanalytic degree and had begun a career as a teacher, an analyst, a writer, and a theorist. Erikson spent some of his youth having an identity crisis. But along the way he was also earning what sociologists call identity capital.

Identity capital is our collection of personal assets. It is the repertoire of individual resources that we assemble over time. These are the investments we make in ourselves, the things we do well enough, or long enough, that they become a part of who we are. Some identity capital goes on a résumé, such as degrees, jobs, test scores, and clubs. Other identity capital is more personal, such as how we speak, where we are from, how we solve problems, how we look. Identity capital is how we build ourselves—bit by bit, over time. Most important, identity capital is what we bring to the adult marketplace. It is the currency we use to metaphorically purchase jobs and relationships and other things we want.

Twentysomethings like Helen imagine that crisis is for now and capital is for later when, in fact, crisis and capital can—and should—go together, like they did for Erikson. Researchers who have looked at how people resolve identity crises have found that lives that are all capital and no crisis—all work and no exploration—feel rigid and conventional. On the other hand, more crisis than capital is a problem too. As the concept of identity crisis caught on in the United States, Erikson himself warned against spending too much time in "disengaged confusion." He was concerned that too many young people were "in danger of becoming irrelevant."

Twentysomethings who take the time to explore and *also* have the nerve to make commitments along the way construct stronger identities. They have higher self-esteem and are more persevering and realistic. This path to identity is associated with a host of positive outcomes, including a clearer sense of self, greater life satisfaction, better stress management, stronger reasoning, and resistance to conformity—all the things Helen wanted.

I encouraged Helen to get some capital. I suggested she start by finding work that could go on a résumé.

"This is my chance to have fun," she resisted. "To be free before real life sets in."

"How is this fun? You're seeing me because you are miserable."

"But I'm *free*!"

"How are you free? You have free time during the day

when most everyone you know is working. You're living on the edge of poverty. You can't do anything with that time."

Helen looked skeptical, as though I were trying to talk her out of her yoga mat and shove a briefcase into her hand. She said, "You're probably one of those people who went straight from college to graduate school."

"I'm not. In fact, I probably went to a much better graduate school because of what I did in between."

Helen's brow furrowed.

I thought for a moment and said, "Do you want to know what I did after college?"

"Yeah, I do," she challenged.

Helen was ready to listen.

The day after I graduated from college, I went to work for Outward Bound. My first job there was as a grunt in logistics. I lived at a base camp in the Blue Ridge Mountains and spent the better part of a year driving vans all over the backcountry, bringing granola and fuel to dirty, haggard groups of students on backpacking trips. I have incredibly fond memories of driving fifteen-passenger vehicles along washboard dirt roads, music blaring from the radio. I was often the only other person these groups would come across for days or weeks at a time. The students were always so happy to see me, because I reminded them that life was still happening elsewhere.

When an instructor job opened up, I jumped at it. I tromped all over the mountains in North Carolina, Maine, and Colorado, sometimes with war veterans and other times with CEOs from Wall Street. I spent one long, hot summer in Boston Harbor on a thirty-foot open sailboat with a bunch of middle-school girls.

My favorite trip—the one I led more than a dozen times—was a twenty-eight-day canoe expedition that ran the full length of the Suwannee River, about 350 miles from the black waters and cypress knees of the Okefenokee Swamp in Georgia, through northern Florida, to the sandy coast of the Gulf of Mexico. The students on these canoe trips were adjudicated youth, the official term for kids who were fondly (but unofficially) called "hoods in the woods." These were either inner-city or deeply rural teenagers who had committed crimes: grand theft, assault and battery, drug dealing—anything short of murder. They were serving their sentence on the river with me.

The work was extraordinarily meaningful, and even more fun. I learned to play a mean game of Spades from the kids who frequented the detention centers. After they zipped themselves into sleeping bags at night, I sat outside the tents and read bedtime stories aloud from chapter books like *Treasure Island*. So often, I got to see these kids just get to be kids, jumping off the riverbanks, their troubles back home nowhere in sight. Reality, though, was never far away. When I was only about twenty-four, I had to tell one adjudicated girl—a fifteen-year-old mother of two—that her own mother had died of AIDS while she was stuck paddling down the Suwannee.

I thought my stint at Outward Bound might last one or two years. Before I noticed, it had been nearly four. Once, on a break between courses, I visited my old college town and saw an undergraduate mentor. I still remember her saying, "What about graduate school?" That was my own dose of reality. I did want to go to graduate school and was growing tired of Outward Bound life. My mentor said if I wanted to go, I needed to do it. "What are you waiting for?" she asked. It seemed I was waiting for someone to tell me to get going. So I did.

The clinical psychology interview circuit is a scene typically loaded with shiny recent grads toting brand-new leather portfolios and wearing ill-fitting suits. When I joined in, I had an ill-fitting suit and a portfolio too. Feeling somewhat out of place having spent the last few years in the woods, I crammed my portfolio with scholarly articles written by the faculty who would probably interview me. I was ready to talk smartly about their clinical trials and to pretend to be passionate about research I might never do.

But no one wanted to talk about that.

Almost invariably, interviewers would glance at my résumé and start excitedly with "Tell me about Outward Bound!" Faculty would introduce themselves to me by saying, "So, you're the Outward Bound girl!" For years to come, even on residency interviews, I spent most of the time answering questions about what happened when kids ran away in the wilderness or whether it was safe to swim in a river with alligators. It really wasn't until I had a doctorate from Berkeley that I started to be known for something else.

I told Helen some of my story. I told her the twentysomething years have a different economy than college. For some, life may be about neatly building on Phi Beta Kappa or an Ivy League degree. More often, identities and careers are made not out of college majors and GPAs but out of a couple of door-opening pieces of identity capital—and I was concerned that Helen wasn't earning any.

No one was going to start off Helen's next job interview by saying, "So tell me about being a nanny!" This gave me pause. If Helen didn't get some capital soon, I knew she could be headed for a lifetime of unhappiness and underemployment.

After my urging to get an over-the-table job, Helen came in to say she was days away from starting work at a coffee shop. Helen also mentioned she had an interview to be a "floater" at a digital animation studio, an interview she wasn't planning to attend. Working at the coffee shop seemed "cool and not corporate" and, besides, she said, she wasn't sure about "just paying dues" and "basically working in the mailroom" at the animation company.

As Helen sat talking about her plan to work at the coffee shop, I tried to keep my jaw from hitting the floor. I had seen what another one of my clients calls "the Starbucks phase" unfold many times. Everything I knew about twentysomething underemployment, and about identity capital, told me that Helen was about to make a bad choice.

At one time or another, most twentysomethings, including my van-driving self, have been underemployed. They work at jobs they are overqualified for or they work only part-time. Some of these jobs are useful stopgaps. They pay the bills while we study for the GMAT or work our way through graduate school. Or, as with Outward Bound, some underemployment generates capital that trumps everything else.

But some underemployment is not a means to an end. Sometimes it is just a way to pretend we aren't working, such as running a ski lift or doing what one executive I know called "the eternal band thing." While these sorts of jobs can be fun, they also signal to future employers a period of lostness. A degree from a university followed by too many unexplained retail and coffee-shop gigs looks backward. Those sorts of jobs can hurt our résumés and even our lives.

The longer it takes to get our footing in work, the more likely we are to become, as one journalist put it, "different and damaged." Research on underemployed twentysomethings tells us that those who are underemployed for as little as nine months tend to be more depressed and less motivated than their peers—*than even their unemployed peers.* But before we decide that unemployment is a better alternative to underemployment, consider this: Twentysomething unemployment is associated with heavy drinking and depression in middle age *even after becoming regularly employed.*

I have seen how this happens. I have watched smart, interesting twentysomethings avoid real jobs in the real world only to drag themselves through years of underemployment, all the while becoming too tired and too alienated to look for something that might actually make them happy. Their dreams seem increasingly distant as people treat them like the name tags they wear.

Economists and sociologists agree that twentysomething work has an inordinate influence on our long-run career success. About two-thirds of lifetime wage growth happens in the first ten years of a career. After that, families and mortgages get in the way of higher degrees and cross-country moves, and salaries rise more slowly. As a twentysomething, it may feel like there are decades ahead to earn more and more but the latest data from the US Census Bureau shows that, on average, salaries peak—and plateau—in our forties.

Twentysomethings who think they have until later to leave unemployment or underemployment behind miss out on moving ahead while they are still traveling light. No matter how smoothly this goes, late bloomers will likely never close the gap between themselves and those who got started earlier. This leaves many thirty- and fortysomethings feeling as if they have ultimately paid a surprisingly high price for a string of random twentysomething jobs. Midlife is when we may realize that our twentysomething choices cannot be undone. Drinking and depression can enter from stage left.

In today's economy, very few people make it to age thirty without some underemployment. So what is a twentysomething to do? Fortunately, not all underemployment is the same. I always advise twentysomethings to take the job with the most capital.

I heard Helen out. Then I told her that working at a coffee shop might have some benefits, like easygoing coworkers or a good discount on beverages. It might even pay more than being a floater. But it had no capital. From the perspective of the sort of identity capital Helen needed, the animation studio was the clear winner. I encouraged Helen to go to the interview, and to think about the floater job not as paying dues but rather as investing in her dream. Learning about the digital art world and making connections in the industry, she could raise capital in untold ways.

"Maybe I should wait for something better to come along?" Helen questioned.

"But something better doesn't just come along. One good piece of capital is *how* you get to better," I said.

We spent our next sessions helping Helen prepare for the interview. Her less-than-stellar pre-med grades, combined with the sting of her parents' reaction to her art major, had left her feeling professionally insecure. But what I haven't yet mentioned about Helen is that she was one of the most personable clients I have ever had. Her college career was imperfect, but Helen had all the pieces of identity capital that don't go on a résumé. She was socially adept. She was an excellent communicator with a quick wit. She was a hard worker. I felt sure that if Helen got herself to the interview, her personality would take it from there.

Helen and the hiring manager had easy conversations about pre-med and freelance photography, and about the fact that his wife had also majored in art at Helen's school. Two weeks later, Helen started at the animation company. After six months, she moved from floating to "a desk." Then, a movie director spent a few weeks at Helen's office, only to decide Helen would make an ideal cinematography assistant. She was brought to Los Angeles, where she now works on movies. This is what she says about her twenties, about the pieces of identity capital that are helping her now:

> I would never have believed it, and it's probably not the best thing to tell someone still in school, but seriously not one person has asked for my GPA since I graduated. So unless you are applying to grad schools, yeah, everyone was right, no one cares. Nor do they care if you did the "wrong" major.
>
> I think about my parents' question: "What are you going to do with your art major?" It makes no sense to me now. No one I know really knew what they wanted to do when they graduated. What people are doing now is usually not something that they'd ever even heard of in

> undergrad. One of my friends is a marine biologist and works at an aquarium. Another is in grad school for epidemiology. I'm in cinematography. None of us knew any of these jobs even existed when we graduated.
>
> That's why I wish I had done more during my first few years out of college. I wish I had pushed myself to take some work leaps or a wider range of jobs. I wish I had experimented—with *work*—in a way I feel I can't right now at almost thirty. I felt a lot of internal pressure to figure it out, but all the thinking I did was really debilitating and unproductive. The one thing I have learned is that you can't think your way through life. The only way to figure out what to do is to do—something.

Whenever I hear from Helen, I think about how different her life might be now if she had gone to work at the coffee shop. Her fun and carefree underemployment would probably quickly have become a depressing and alienating experience, one that might have dragged on longer than expected just as other twentysomethings were going to, say, work in digital animation.

She wouldn't have been at the coffee shop forever, of course. But she also would not have been swooped up by a director, because any director ordering coffee from her would have seen her as a clerk, not as someone who might be relevant to the film industry. On it would go from there. Five or ten years later, the difference between coffee-shop Helen and digital-animation Helen could be remarkable.

Sadly remarkable. Helen's life got going when she used the bits of capital she had to get the next piece of capital she wanted—and it didn't hurt that she and the hiring manager's wife shared the same alma mater.

That's almost always the way it works.

Weak Ties

[Those] deeply enmeshed in [a close-knit group] may never become aware of the fact that their lives do not actually depend on what happens within the group but on forces far beyond their perception.

—Rose Coser, sociologist

Yes is how you get your first job, and your next job, and your spouse, and even your kids. Even if it's a bit edgy, a bit out of your comfort zone, saying yes means you will do something new, meet someone new, and make a difference.

—Eric Schmidt, executive chairman of Google

A few summers ago, a big box showed up at my house. The return address on the label was a major publishing house in New York City. The box was addressed to me.

I was prepping two courses for the fall and had ordered some textbooks to look over but, when I opened the box, I found not textbooks but about a hundred paperback books—some fiction, some nonfiction, some academic, some popular. The invoice inside listed the name of an editor. I put the box of books in the middle of my dining-room table and friends who came to the house would ask about it: How did I find time to do so much reading? Had I lost my mind? No one found my explanation of "it came in the mail and I don't know why" very satisfying.

After some time, I made an attempt to follow up. I e-mailed the editor on the invoice to let her know I might have a box intended for her. She discovered the books were sent to me in error but said to enjoy them. I thanked her, and we exchanged a couple of e-mails about choosing textbooks. Some months later, she asked if I would be interested in writing an instructor's guide for a book she was editing; I said sure. At the next barbecue at my home, the big box of books was still on the dining-room table. I told friends to please take home whatever titles looked appealing. It made a good story.

About a year after the box of books arrived, I started to want to write a book of my own. My private practice and classes were filled with twentysomethings who sincerely wanted, and needed, help moving forward. I envisioned a book that pulled together what I knew about the twenties from teaching and research and clinical work, a book twentysomethings anywhere could read.

I borrowed a sample book proposal from a distant colleague, and I went to work on the project in my spare hours. When I finished the proposal, I asked the editor whose books I had accidentally received if she would give me her impressions. She read it and quickly introduced me to interested parties. Soon, the book had a publisher.

I had never met the editor with the box of books or the publisher who ultimately acquired my book. I had only once met the colleague whose proposal I used as a model. No one had any reason to give me preferential treatment and, business is business, so no one did. This book, like most things in adulthood, came to be because of what is called the strength of weak ties.

The Strength of Weak Ties

The urban tribe is overrated. For the past decade or so, there has been much talk about the urban tribe, or the makeshift family that has come to the fore as twentysomethings spend more years on their own. Sitcoms and movies tout the value of the tribe, the fun of having a place to go with that store-bought pumpkin pie when we can't make it "home-home" for Thanksgiving, how nice it feels to have a group to call our own.

Without a doubt, these friends play a crucial, supportive role for many twentysomethings, and they provide lots of good times. Essentially the college buddies of the twentysomething years, the urban tribe, are the people we meet up with on the weekend. They give us rides to the airport. We vent about bad dates and breakups over burritos and beer.

With all the attention paid to the urban tribe, however, many twentysomethings have limited themselves to huddling together with like-minded peers. Some are in almost constant contact with the same few people. But while the urban tribe helps us survive, it does not help us thrive. The urban tribe may bring us soup when we are sick, but it is the people we hardly know—those who never make it into our tribe—who will swiftly and dramatically change our lives for the better.

In work that predates Facebook by more than twenty-five years, sociologist and Stanford professor Mark Granovetter conducted one of the first and most famous studies of social networks. Granovetter was curious about how networks foster social mobility, about how the people in our lives lead to new opportunities. Surveying workers in a Boston suburb who had recently changed jobs, Granovetter found it wasn't close friends and family—presumably those most invested in helping—who were the most valuable during the job hunt. Rather, more than three-quarters of new jobs had come from leads from contacts who were seen only "occasionally" or "rarely." This finding led Granovetter to write a groundbreaking paper titled "The Strength of Weak Ties" about the unique value of people we do not know well.

According to Granovetter, not all relationships—or ties—are created equal. Some are weak and some are strong, and the strength of a tie increases with time and experience. The more we have been around someone, the stronger the tie because, likely, we have shared experiences and confidences. In childhood, strong ties are family and best friends. In the twentysomething years, strong ties grow to include the urban tribe, roommates, partners, and other close friends.

Weak ties are the people we have met, or are connected to somehow, but do not currently know well. Maybe they are the coworkers we rarely talk with or the neighbor we only say hello to. We all have acquaintances we keep meaning to go out with but never do, and friends we lost touch with years ago. Weak ties are also our former employers or professors and any other associations who have not been promoted to close friends.

But why are some people promoted while others are not? A century of research in sociology—and thousands of years of Western thought—show that "similarity breeds connection." Birds of a feather flock together because of homophily, or "love of the same." From the schoolyard to the boardroom, people are more likely to form close relationships with those most like themselves. As a result, a cluster of strong ties—such as the urban tribe or even an online social network—is typically an incestuous group. A homogeneous clique.

Here we get to what another sociologist, Rose Coser, called the "weakness of strong ties," or how our close friends hold us back. Our strong ties feel comfortable and familiar but, other than support, they may have little to offer. They are usually too similar—even too similarly stuck—to provide more than sympathy. They often don't know any more about jobs or relationships than we do.

Weak ties feel too different or, in some cases, literally too far away to be close friends. But that's the point. Because they're not just figures in an already ingrown cluster, weak ties give us access to something fresh. They know things and people that we don't know. Information and opportunity spread farther and faster through weak ties than through close friends because weak ties have fewer overlapping contacts. Weak ties are like bridges you cannot see all the way across, so there is no telling where they might lead.

It's not just who and what our ties know that matters. It is how we communicate with them as well. Because close-knit groups of strong ties are usually so similar, they tend to use a simple, encoded way of communicating known as restricted speech. Economical but incomplete, restricted speech relies on in-crowd colloquialisms and shortcuts to say more with less. Texters all know that FTW means "for the win" just as businesspeople know that JIT stands for "just in time."

But in-group members share more than slang and vocabulary. They share assumptions about one another and the world. They may have gone to the same schools or have the same ideas about love. Our strong ties probably all watch Glenn Beck or Rachel Maddow or Stephen Colbert—or they decidedly do *not.* Whatever the particular sources of sameness, hanging out with them can limit who and what we know, how we talk, and ultimately how we think.

Weak ties, on the other hand, force us to communicate from a place of difference, to use what is called elaborated speech. Unlike restricted speech, which presupposes similarities between the speaker and the listener, elaborated speech does not presume that the listener thinks in the same way or knows the same information. We need to be more thorough when we talk to weak ties, and this requires more organization and reflection. There are fewer tags, such as "ya know," and sentences are less likely to trail off at the end. Whether we are talking about career ideas or our thoughts on love, we have to make our case more fully. In this way, weak ties promote, and sometimes even force, thoughtful growth and change.

Meet Cole and Betsy.

Cole burst out of college toward his twentysomething years like a middle schooler runs toward summer on the last day of school. As an engineering major, he'd spent his undergraduate years solving equations while it seemed everyone else was having fun. His twenties were Cole's chance to have a good time. He took a low-key job within a firm of surveyors, preferring to clock in and clock out without thinking much about work. He moved into an apartment with a group of guys he met, some of whom had not gone to college at all. Over some years, this became Cole's urban tribe:

> We'd sit around and drink and talk about how much we hated work or how the job market sucked. We were anti doing anything. We were all just preaching to the choir. None of those guys was thinking about a real career, so I wasn't either. I was part of the cool club, I guess you could say. I wasn't thinking about anything except the next basketball game I was going to or whatever. That's what I thought everybody else was doing too because that's what everyone I saw *was* doing.
>
> Then sometimes I'd hear about somebody I knew from college who had made bank starting some business or who had some awesome job at Google or something. And I'd think, "*That guy?* That's not fair. I was busting my ass in college while he was majoring in anthropology." It was like the fact that he'd been doing something with his twenties while I'd been screwing around didn't mean anything. I didn't want to admit it, but after a while I wanted to be one of those guys who was doing something with his life. I just didn't know how.

Cole's sister dragged him to her roommate's thirtieth birthday party. Uncomfortably surrounded by people who were older and more successful, Cole passed the time talking to a young sculptor he met, a client of mine named Betsy.

Betsy was tired of dating the same kind of person. It seemed like the moment she broke up with one boyfriend who "didn't have his shit together," she started dating another guy who didn't either. Eventually, Betsy came to therapy to examine why she was drawn to this sort of man again and again. But having more insight about it did not change the fact that she kept meeting the same fun and unambitious guys. "I can't get a decent date," she said.

Betsy didn't want to be at the party any more than Cole did. She'd met the birthday girl in a spin class a couple of years earlier and had been declining her Evites ever since. In an effort to meet new people, this time Betsy replied "Yes." She took a cab to the party, wondering why she was subjecting herself to this.

When Betsy met Cole there was a spark, but she was ambivalent. Cole was clearly smart and well educated, but he didn't seem to be doing much about it. They had some nice dinner dates, which seemed promising. Then, after sleeping over one night and watching Cole wake up at eleven a.m. and grab his skateboard, Betsy felt less bullish.

What she didn't know was that ever since he'd started spending time with Betsy, Cole had regained some of his old drive. He saw the way she wanted to work on her sculptures even on the weekend, how she and her friends loved to get together to talk about their projects and their plans. He eyed a posting on Craigslist for a challenging tech job at a high-profile start-up, but he felt his résumé was too shabby to apply.

Cole remembered that an old high school friend, someone he saw about once a year around town, worked at the start-up. He got in touch, and this friend put in a good word about Cole. After a handful of interviews with different people in the company, he was offered the position. The hiring manager told Cole he had been chosen for three reasons: his engineering degree suggested he knew how to work hard on technical projects, his personality seemed like a good fit for the group, and the twentysomething who vouched for him was well liked in the company. The rest, the manager said, he could learn on the job.

This radically altered Cole's career path. He learned software development at a dot-com on the leading edge. A few years later, Cole moved over and up as a director of development at another start-up because, by then, the capital he'd gained at the dot-com could speak for itself.

Nearly ten years later, Cole and Betsy are married. She runs a gallery co-op. He's a CIO. They have a happy life and gladly give much of the credit to Cole's friend from high school and to the woman with the Evites. Weak ties changed their lives.

When I encourage twentysomethings to draw on the strength of weak ties, there is often a fair amount of resistance: "I hate networking" or "I want to get a job on my own" or "That's not my style" are common reactions. I get it, but that doesn't change the fact that, as we look for jobs or relationships or opportunities of any kind, it is the people we know the least well who will be the most transformative. New things almost always come from outside your inner circle. And twentysomethings who won't use their weak ties fall behind twentysomethings like these, who have this to say:

> Networking, using contacts, whatever, is not a bad thing. I never really was overly worried about it, but I have some friends who always were so stressed about working somewhere where a family member helped them get the job. I work in one of the top three companies in my industry, and literally I know only one person who actually got a job there without knowing someone. Everyone got it because they know somebody.

> I hate randomly calling people I don't know. Hate, hate, hate it. But my dad met someone at a holiday party who used to work at the company where I am now and he told him I was interested in the fashion industry. I finally called this person just to get some information, and he passed along my résumé. That is how I got the interview.

> There was a hospital where I wanted to work, and I kept looking for them to post some job openings, but they never did. I finally called a friend of mine who worked there. I'd put that off because I wasn't sure if that was wrong or if I'd be putting her in a bad spot. But right away she gave me the name of someone to call at the hospital. When I did call, they were about to post a job. I got it before they even posted. Everything

> can change in a day. Especially if you put yourself out there.
>
> I think sometimes people think, "I don't know anyone and everyone else does," but people would be surprised at the untapped resources they have. Alumni networks from college and high schools can be really helpful, and if there's not an official network, go through the Facebook group or LinkedIn group for your school. Look through and see where people work. If there is someone who does something you want to do, call or e-mail them for an "informational interview." That is what everybody ultimately does.

Most twentysomethings yearn for a feeling of community, and they cling to their strong ties to feel more connected. Ironically, being enmeshed with a group can actually enhance feelings of alienation, because we—and our tribe—become insular and detached. Over time, our initial feeling of being part of a group becomes a sense of disconnection with the larger world.

True interconnectedness rests not on texting best friends at one a.m., but on reaching out to weak ties that make a difference in our lives even though they don't have to. When weak ties help, the communities around us—even the adult community that twentysomethings are warily in the process of entering—seem less impersonal and impenetrable. Suddenly, the world seems smaller and easier to navigate. The more we know about the way things work, the more we feel a part of things.

Favors are how things begin. Take Benjamin Franklin, for instance.

The Ben Franklin Effect

In the late 1700s, Benjamin Franklin was a state-level politician in Pennsylvania. He wanted to win over a fellow legislator and described the following in his autobiography:

> I did not... aim at gaining his favour by paying any servile respect to him but, after some time, took this other method. Having heard that he had in his library a very certain scarce and curious book I wrote a note to him expressing my desire of perusing that book and requesting he would do me the favour of lending it to me for a few days. He sent it immediately and I returned it in about a week with another note expressing strongly my sense of favour. When we next met in the House he spoke to me (which he had never done before), and with great civility; and ever after he manifested a readiness to serve me on all occasions, so that we became great friends and our friendship continued to his death. This is another instance of the truth of an old maxim I had learned, which says, "He that hath once done you a kindness will be more ready to do you another than he whom you yourself have obliged."

We imagine that if people like us, then they do us favors because this is how it works in the urban tribe. But the Ben

Franklin effect, and subsequent empirical studies, show it works the other way around with people we know less well.

If weak ties do favors for us, they start to like us. Then they become even more likely to grant us additional favors in the future. Franklin decided that if he wanted to get someone on his side, he ought to ask for a favor. And he did.

The Ben Franklin effect shows that, while attitudes influence behavior, behavior can also shape attitudes. If we do a favor for someone, we come to believe we like that person. This liking leads back to another favor, and so on. A close variant of what is called the foot-in-the-door technique, or the strategy of making small requests before larger ones, the Ben Franklin effect tells us that one favor begets more favors and, over time, small favors beget larger ones.

What often isn't discussed about the Ben Franklin effect is a question twentysomethings wonder about a lot: Why would a person—especially maybe an older or more successful person—help in the first place? How did Franklin get his foot in the door with that *first* favor?

It's simple. It's good to be good. There is a "helper's high" that comes from being generous. In numerous studies, altruism has been linked to happiness, health, and longevity—*as long as the help we give is not a burden.* Most people remember starting out themselves, being helped by those who were further along. Because of this, there is a reserve of goodwill toward twentysomethings. Part of aging well is helping others, and twentysomethings who turn to weak ties for help give them a chance to do good and feel good—unless what they ask for is overwhelming.

So let's talk about that.

Sometimes twentysomethings reach out to weak ties

with amorphous career aspirations, hoping other professionals can help them make up their minds about what to do with their lives. These sorts of favors may not overwhelm the capabilities of successful others, but they can overwhelm their calendars or their roles. It simply takes too much time to type a multiparagraph reply to an e-mail about which graduate degree someone should pursue. And it's really not for a weak tie to say whether you should be a social worker or a folk singer.

As a human resources professional said to me, "I have people make appointments to learn about future open positions at our company, and they come in and do this..." She sat back in her chair and folded her hands in her lap. Then she continued, "I think to myself, '*You* called this meeting. Have some good questions. Don't just ask how long I've been at the company to make conversation until I can tell you what to do with your life.'"

Let's look more closely at the favor Franklin requested. He didn't have a messenger deliver to the legislator a scroll that read "Peanut soup at the tavern???"—perhaps the eighteenth-century equivalent of an e-mail with the subject heading "Coffee???" or "A quick chat???" Franklin knew this sort of overture would seem dangerously vague to a busy professional. He was more intentional—and strategic—than that.

Franklin did research on his target and found out the legislator's areas of expertise. He presented himself as a serious person with a need that matched. He made himself interesting. He made himself relevant. And he asked for a clearly defined favor: the use of a book.

I would advise the same approach today as you ask your

own weak ties for letters of recommendation, suggestions or introductions, or well-planned informational interviews: Make yourself interesting. Make yourself relevant. Do your homework so you know precisely what you want or need. Then, respectfully, ask for it. Some weak ties will say no. More than you think will say yes. The fastest route to something new is one phone call, one e-mail, one box of books, one favor, one thirtieth birthday party.

I once had a fortune cookie that read A WISE MAN MAKES HIS OWN LUCK. Perhaps the single best thing we can do to make our own luck in our twenties is say yes to our weak ties or give them a reason to say yes to us. Research shows that our social networks *narrow* across adulthood, as careers and families become busier and more defined. So—even and especially as we job-hop and move cross-country and change roommates and spend our weekends about town—this is the time to be connecting, not just with the same people having the same conversations about how work is lame or how there are no good men out there, but with those who might see things a little differently. Weak ties are the people who will better your life right now—and again and again in the years to come—if you have the courage to know what you want.

The Unthought Known

Uncertainty will always be part of the taking-charge process.
—Harold Geneen, businessman

The search of youth is not for all-permissibility, but rather for new ways of directly facing up to what truly counts.
—Erik Erikson, psychoanalyst

Ian told me his twentysomething years were like being in the middle of the ocean, like this vast, unmarked body of water. He couldn't see land in any direction, so he didn't know which way to go. He felt overwhelmed by the prospect that he could swim anywhere or do anything. He was equally paralyzed by the fact that he didn't know which of the anythings would work out. Tired and hopeless at age twenty-five, he said he was treading water to stay alive.

As I listened to Ian, I started to feel a bit hopeless myself. I try to, as psychologists say, "meet my clients where they are," but Ian's ocean metaphor was a real problem. When I thought of myself out there with him, with so many directions that seemed the same, I couldn't come up with a good solution either.

"How *do* people get out of the ocean?" I asked Ian, wondering if he had some sense of how he might stop treading water.

"I don't know," he said, turning his head as he thought intently. "I would say you pick a direction and start swimming. But you can't tell one way from the other, so you can't pick. You can't even tell if you're swimming toward something, so why would you use up all your energy going the wrong way? I guess all you can do is hope someone comes along in a boat or something," Ian said, almost with relief.

There is a certain terror that goes along with saying "My life is up to me." It is scary to realize there's no magic, you can't just wait around, no one can really rescue you, and you have to do something. Not knowing what you want to do with your life—or not at least having some ideas about what to do next—is a defense against that terror. It is a resistance to admitting that the possibilities are not endless. It is a way of pretending that now doesn't matter. Being confused about choices is nothing more than hoping that maybe there is a way to get through life without taking charge.

Rather than take charge, Ian hoped someone would come along, pick him up, and carry him off in a predetermined direction. It happens all the time. Maybe Ian would hop aboard with a group of friends or with some girlfriend. He'd go their way for a while and be distracted from his life a bit longer. But I knew how that would play out. He'd wake up one day in a far-off land, working in a job or living in a place that had nothing at all to do with Ian. He would be a world away from the life he would suddenly realize he wanted.

With his ocean metaphor, Ian was pretending there was no particular life he wanted to live. It was like he had no past and no future, and no reason for going one way or the other. He wasn't reflecting on the years he had lived so far, and neither was he thinking through the years that were ahead. As he said, this made action impossible. Because Ian didn't know that twentysomethings who make choices are happier than those who tread water, he kept himself confused. This was easy to do.

Ian hung out with an indecisive crowd. At the bike shop where he worked, his friends assured him he didn't need to make decisions yet—"We're not!" they cheered. They had long discussions on the job about never settling and about never selling out, yet there they were, settling for underemployment and selling out their futures. I suspected Ian was in my office because somehow he knew these conversations were full of unintentional lies.

When Ian turned to his parents about his vectorless life in the ocean, he heard other lies. His mom and dad said, "You're the best! The sky is the limit!" They reminded him he could do anything he set his mind to. They didn't understand that this undefined encouragement was not helpful. It led less to courage than it did to confusion.

Twentysomethings like Ian were raised on abstract commands—"Follow your dreams!" "Reach for the stars!"—but they often don't know much about how to get these things done. They don't know how to get what they want or, sometimes, even what they want. As Ian put it to me, almost desperately, "My mom goes on to me and everybody else about how great I am and how proud she is of me, and I want to say: *For what?* What exactly stands out about me?"

Far from narcissistically lapping up his mother's praise, Ian had long sensed that her words were too generic to mean much. He felt hoodwinked—and with good reason. Life isn't limitless, and neither was Ian. Twentysomethings often say they wish they had fewer choices but, at the moment, Ian didn't have as many choices as he'd heard he did. And the longer he waited to get going, the fewer the options were going to be.

"I want you to come back next week," I said. "When you do, we're getting out of the ocean. It's not the right metaphor. We're going shopping for jam instead."

There is a classic study in psychology known as the jam experiment. The jam experiment was conducted by a researcher named Sheena Iyengar who, then at Stanford University, had the idea that the local grocery store would be an excellent place to understand how people make choices. Iyengar's research assistants posed as jam suppliers and set up sampling tables at a gourmet store. In one condition of the experiment, six flavors of jam were available for tasting: peach, black cherry, red currant, marmalade, kiwi, and lemon curd. In another condition, twenty-four flavors of jam were featured: the six flavors just mentioned plus eighteen others. In both conditions, customers who tasted the jam could then use a coupon to buy a jar at lower cost.

The key finding in the study was that the twenty-four-flavor table attracted more attention yet it resulted in fewer buyers. Shoppers flocked to the exciting array, yet most became overwhelmed and dropped out of buying jam altogether. Only 3 percent of those who visited the twenty-four-flavor table went on to buy jam. In contrast, shoppers who visited the six-flavor table were more able to decide which jar was right for them, with about 30 percent leaving the store with jam in hand.

The next week, I told Ian about the jam experiment and wondered aloud about whether he felt too overwhelmed by life's purported possibilities to pick something.

"I *do* feel overwhelmed by the idea that I could do anything with my life," he said.

"Then let's get concrete. Let's talk about choosing jam," I offered.

"Am I at the six-flavor table or the twenty-four-flavor table?" he asked.

"That is an excellent question. I think part of making any decision in your twenties is realizing there is no twenty-four-flavor table. It's a myth."

"Why is it a myth?"

"Twentysomethings hear they are standing in front of a boundless array of choices. Being told you can do anything or go anywhere is like being in the ocean you described. It's like standing in front of the twenty-four-flavor table. But I have yet to meet a twentysomething who has twenty-four truly viable options. Each person is choosing from his or her own six-flavor table, at best."

Ian looked at me blankly, so I went on.

"You've spent more than two decades shaping who you are. You have experiences, interests, strengths, weaknesses, diplomas, hang-ups, priorities. You didn't just this moment drop onto the planet or, as you put it, into the ocean. The past twenty-five years are relevant. You're standing in front of six flavors of jam and you know something about whether you prefer kiwi or black cherry."

"I just want things to be great," Ian said. "I just want things to work out."

"You're keeping it vague," I challenged. "You're avoiding knowing what you know."

"So you think I already know what I should do?"

"I think you know something. I think there are realities. Let's start there."

"So this is like the lottery question," he said.

"What's the lottery question?" I asked.

"You know," Ian continued, "it's when you ask yourself what you would do with your life if you won the lottery. Then you know what you really want to do."

"That's not the right question," I countered. "That's not about reality. The lottery question might get you thinking about what you would do if talent and money didn't matter. But they do. The question twentysomethings need to ask themselves is what they would do with their lives if they *didn't* win the lottery. What might you be able to do well enough to support the life you want? And what might you enjoy enough that you won't mind working at it in some form or another for years to come?"

"I don't know anything about that."

"That cannot be true."

Over the next months, Ian told me about his experiences at work and in school. For a long time, I just listened. Ian talked, and we *both* listened to what he said. After a while, I reflected back specific information about what I heard and saw. There was an early interest in drawing. A childhood love for LEGOs and building. An architecture major he started, but didn't finish, because it felt too archaic. He earned his degree in cognitive science because he liked technology and perception. I saw Ian talk easily about his wish to create products of some kind.

Eventually, Ian thought through all of the options that seemed available to him. He assembled six tangible flavors of jam, six things he might do next.

"I could keep working at the bike shop, but it is kind of gnawing at me. I know it's the wrong thing to do. My manager is in his forties and something about that really bothers me...."

"I could go to law school. My parents are always telling me I should do that. But I don't want to take the LSAT and I hate reading and I hate writing and I guess there's a lot of that in law school...."

"Now that so much design is happening online, that interests me. The interface between design and technology interests me. I applied to a digital design apprentice program in D.C. a couple of years ago. It was at a company that takes a lot of postgrads and sort of develops and launches them. I wanted to do that but I didn't get in...."

"I could take Arabic lessons and do something with, you know, international relations or something, and maybe get sent overseas somewhere. But that's just an idea. I enrolled in a class a while back but I never went...."

"I could go visit my buddy in Cambodia to buy some more time, but my parents are getting sick of me doing that...."

"I could go to St. Louis and hang out with my old girlfriend. She watches *Grey's Anatomy* all the time and says we should both get post-bacs. But I only took two hard science classes in college, and I didn't do so well in them. Anyway, this probably sounds bad, but I cannot even deal with her until I get somewhere with this whole work thing on my own."

(It didn't sound bad. Work before love. I'd heard that from twentysomethings—and especially twentysomething men—many times before.)

By thinking through his actual options, Ian stumbled onto a twentysomething version of what psychoanalyst Christopher Bollas calls the unthought known. Unthought knowns are those things we know about ourselves but forget somehow. These are the dreams we have lost sight of or the truths we sense but don't say out loud. We may be afraid of acknowledging the unthought known to other people because we are afraid of what they might think. Even more often, we fear what the unthought known will then mean for ourselves and our lives.

Ian pretended that not knowing what to do was the hard part when, somewhere inside, I think he knew that making a choice about something is when the *real* uncertainty begins. The more terrifying uncertainty is wanting something but not knowing *how* to get it. It is working toward something even though there is no sure thing. When we make choices, we open ourselves up to hard work and failure and heartbreak, so sometimes it feels easier not to know, not to choose, and not to do.

But it isn't.

"Ian, the first day I met you, you said you were in the middle of the ocean. I got the impression there was nothing in particular you wanted to do, like you had no idea what you wanted. You weren't letting yourself know your own thoughts. There is something you want. You want to try something in digital design."

"I don't know..." Ian hedged.

Here came all of the questions that Ian's not-knowing had been defending against.

"But I don't know how to get into a job in digital design...."

"I do," I said.

"Then what if I start and I change my mind?"

"Then you'll do something else. This isn't the only jar of jam you'll ever get to buy."

"But if I go for it and it fails, I will have spent it. That choice will be gone."

"It won't be gone. It will be better informed. Important questions remain: Can you make a living? Will you like the work? These are things you need to find out."

"I get hung up thinking I should know if this is going to work out if I'm going try it. It feels safer not to pick."

"Not making choices isn't safe. The consequences are just further away in time, like in your thirties or forties."

"I just keep thinking my parents will say I should be doing something more prestigious like law. Or I think I should do something more interesting like the Arabic thing. I don't want my life to be a jar of jam. That's boring."

"That's also what gets in the way of knowing what you know and acting on it," I said. "It's called the tyranny of the should."

More on Ian later.

My Life Should Look Better on Facebook

The best is the enemy of the good.

—Voltaire, writer/philosopher

If we only wanted to be happy, it would be easy; but we want to be happier than other people, which is almost always difficult, since we think them happier than they are.

—Charles de Montesquieu, writer/philosopher

I think I'm having a nervous breakdown," Talia said as she burst into tears.

"A nervous breakdown," I said, never having even met her before. "Can you tell me what that looks like?"

Talia caught me up in a flood of words and sobs.

"I graduated from college almost two years ago. For some ridiculous reason, I left school thinking I was about to embark on the time of my life. I had driven myself crazy with perfectionism for almost fifteen years and I viewed the uncharted life after college as the ultimate escape from this torture. Sadly, the endless nights of partying and the freedom to do whatever I wanted haven't turned out to be quite as fabulous as I expected."

She fumbled for Kleenex in her purse.

"Within months, I was living a lonely and depressing life in San Francisco. The majority of my friends are dispersed throughout the country and the one close friend I was living with suddenly did a one-eighty and abandoned me. I spend my days browsing Craigslist for jobs and going to the gym. I feel like I'm breaking down. I can't sleep. I'm crying all the time. My mom thinks I need medication."

I listened some more.

"And these are supposed to be the best years of my life!" Talia implored.

"They are?" I asked.

"Yeah," she said, this time seeming a bit unsure.

"In my experience, these are the most uncertain and some of the most difficult years of life."

"Why doesn't anybody tell you that?!"

"It may not help much, but I'm telling you now," I said.

"I feel like an incredible failure," Talia continued. "In school there was a formula. It was pretty easy to figure out what to do so you'd know where you stand. You'd know you were living up to your potential. Sometimes I think I should just go to graduate school because it would sound better and I could get A's again. I don't know how to get an A in my twenties. I feel like I am failing for the first time."

"What would an A in your twenties even mean?" I wondered aloud.

"I don't know. That's the problem. I just feel like I shouldn't be less-than."

"Less than what?"

"I think I thought life should be grand, in whatever way you define grand. Grand was A's when I was in school. Then I thought maybe it would be some amazing job or guy. I felt like my life should be Big! Love should be full of grand gestures. Work should make people say Wow! But it doesn't. None of it does."

"Of course not," I said.

"But look at Facebook! These are supposed to be my glory days!"

You might be surprised by the number of hours a week I spend hearing about Facebook. Many of my clients feel their lives on Facebook are evaluated, even judged, daily. They reluctantly admit they spend hours posting pictures and comments, flipping through them again and again, trying to see their Facebook pages as others will. They imagine their ex-girlfriends reacting to how they look now. They wonder whether the mean girls they used to know will think they have cool-looking friends. One of my clients laughs at what he calls his Facebook "self-advertisement." When clients make this Facebook confession, they feel like the only ones who do this.

They aren't.

Facebook and other networking sites have the power to help people feel more connected and less alone. Some 90 percent of users say they use Facebook to stay in touch with longtime acquaintances, and 50 percent have found out something important about their friends this way. This can be especially helpful in our twenties because, as Talia noted, these are some of the most far-flung years of our lives. Facebook can help twentysomething life feel more coherent and less random. So why do many twentysomethings secretly, and not so secretly, hate Facebook?

For many, Facebook is less about looking up friends than it is about looking *at* friends. Research tells us that, on average, Facebook users spend more time examining others' pages than adding content to their own. The site's most frequent visitors—most often females who post and share photos and who receive status updates—use the site for "social surveillance." These social investigators usually aren't getting in touch or staying in touch with friends as much as they are checking up on them. And my clients are right: Judging and evaluating *are* involved. In one study, nearly four hundred participants examined mock-up Facebook pages and rated web-page owners for attractiveness, only to decide that the best-looking owners were the ones with the best-looking friends.

Despite its revolutionary promises, Facebook can turn our everyday lives into that wedding we have all heard about: the one where the bride chooses her prettiest friends, not her best friends, to be bridesmaids. It can feel like a popularity contest where being Liked is what matters, being the best is the only respectable option, how our partners look is more important than how they act, the race to get married is on, and we have to be clever all the time. It can be just another place, not to be, but to *seem*.

Rather than a way of catching up, Facebook can be one

more way of *keeping* up. What's worse is that now we feel the need to keep up not just with our closest friends and neighbors, but with hundreds of others whose manufactured updates continually remind us of how glorious life should be.

Recently a twenty-six-year-old client said to me, "*All* of my friends are having babies. It makes me feel so behind." Statistically this did not seem possible, so I asked which friends: Whom had she ever mentioned in sessions who was now having a baby? She said, "Oh, none of those friends. Just a ton of the nine hundred other people I wouldn't even know about without Facebook updates." Or a male client said to me, "I feel pretty good about how my career is going until I look on Facebook and I see what other people are doing."

Most twentysomethings know better than to compare their lives to celebrity microblogs, yet they treat Facebook images and posts from their peers as real. We don't recognize that most everyone is keeping their troubles hidden. This underestimation of how much other twentysomethings are struggling makes everything feel like an upward social comparison, one where our not-so-perfect lives look low compared to the high life everyone else seems to be living. This leaves twentysomethings like Talia feeling not empowered and connected, but helpless and alone.

When Talia went online, the jobs she saw on Craigslist didn't match the parties and the lives she saw on Facebook. "It makes me feel depressed and stuck because I'm not saving orphans like everybody else," she said.

"Do you want to be saving orphans?" I asked.

"I want to be reaching my potential."

"What does saving orphans have to do with *your*

potential? Do you have some sort of interest or experience in being a humanitarian?"

"Not really."

The Search for Glory and the Tyranny of the Should

Each person has an inherent urge to grow toward his or her potential, much in the way an acorn becomes a tree. But because we all aren't acorns and won't all be oaks, there is bound to be confusion about what exactly growing toward our potential means. Some twentysomethings dream too small, not understanding that their twentysomething choices matter and are, in fact, shaping the years ahead. Others dream too big, fueled more by fantasies about limitless possibilities than by experience. Part of realizing our potential is recognizing how our particular gifts and limitations fit with the world around us. We *realize* where our authentic potential actually lies.

Working toward our potential becomes what developmental theorist Karen Horney called a search for glory when, somehow, we learn more about what is ideal than about what is real. Maybe we feel the cultural press to be an engineer before we find out what exactly that entails. Or our parents tell us more about what we should be like than what we are like. Or Facebook suggests that our twentysomething lives ought to look a lot better than they do. Scrambling after ideals, we become alienated from what is true about ourselves and the world.

Sometimes my clients are unclear about whether they are striving toward their potential or are on a search for glory, but a search for glory is pretty easy to spot. Any search for glory is propelled by what Horney called the tyranny of the should. Listening to Talia talk, it was difficult *not* to notice the "shoulds" and "supposed to's" that littered her sentences: Work should be Wow! She should be in graduate school. Her life should look better than it did.

Shoulds can masquerade as high standards or lofty goals, but they are not the same. Goals direct us from the inside, but shoulds are paralyzing judgments from the outside. Goals feel like authentic dreams while shoulds feel like oppressive obligations. Shoulds set up a false dichotomy between either meeting an ideal or being a failure, between perfection or settling. The tyranny of the should even pits us against our own best interests.

Contrary to what we see and hear, reaching your potential isn't even something that usually happens in your twenties—it happens in your thirties or forties or fifties. And starting that process often means doing what doesn't look so good, such as carting granola around in vans or choosing a starter job. As a twentysomething client who works on a trading desk recently said to me, "These are the years when I put the hard work in, right?" Or as another who works in journalism asked, "I figure I'll be fetching coffee for higher-ups at the office at least until I'm thirty, right?"

Right.

Talia and I spent some time talking about what was *real.* An unemployment rate of nearly 10 percent. Median starting salaries for college grads hovering around $30,000, and median student debt hovering at about the same. Only about half of recent graduates working in jobs that require college degrees. The danger of being unemployed for too long. What her actual friends' lives were really like.

With student loans and financial woes from childhood, Talia needed a job—with or without the Wow!—and she knew it. She also needed to find ways to feel good about herself without A's, because, fortunately and unfortunately, those days were gone.

Talia's hard work in college was not for nothing. At a time when so many have trouble finding jobs, soon she was hired as a marketing analyst. Her job was difficult, but she saw it was the friction between herself and her work that sparked her real potential. In school, Talia had been good at following directions, but at work she became more directed on her own. Her ease with people grew in meetings and on phone calls, and she found she had a real knack for coordinating teams and projects. Collapsing on the couch with a Lean Cuisine after a long day at work wasn't what she expected from her twenties, yet she felt happier and more successful than ever before.

This is how she explained that change:

> For a while, I worried I was selling myself short or not reaching my potential by not getting a Fulbright or going to graduate school, even though I knew that those sorts of things hadn't made me happy. I knew I didn't really want to do those things. But it was like what I was doing wasn't any good because it wasn't the best thing I saw people doing. I knew I had to stop worrying about how life was supposed to look, because it wasn't pretty.
>
> I stopped thinking about whether what I was doing was below me. I learned to not worry about

> how to make it to the next level and just focus on the job at hand. If they were willing to let me do it, I was willing to try. I think the fact that I never felt like I was better than those around me, and that I was just focused on learning and getting results, is what has led me to better and better things at my company.
>
> I guess you could say I gained humility. I saw that bigness came from investing in what I had, from taking part in what was in front of me. I have been able to discover a career field I never would have considered and I have learned to appreciate my talents. I have more courage and self-confidence. I have a lot more perseverance. So far my twenties have been a great, but rude, awakening. I'm even grateful for the internal transformation I've undergone.

Talia's search for glory might have ended at school and at work but, nearly two years later, the tyranny of the should continued after hours. Weeknights, she sat home and clicked through the photos of the parties she was apparently missing. She apologized to her friends for not going out more, though she'd grown progressively bored by spending her weekends talking to people who were drunk. One afternoon she came in crying, looking a lot like she did the first time I saw her in tears.

"Aren't I supposed to be traveling in France or something right now, like for three years?" she asked with equal parts anger and confusion.

"Sort of... but sort of *not*," I said slowly, trying to unwind in my mind what could have raised this. With her tailored shirt and tiny handbag, Talia didn't look like she would enjoy traveling for three years. And how would she pay for it?

"Is going to France for three years what you want to be doing?" I asked.

"No," she sniffled, "but shouldn't I be having my own *Eat, Pray, Love*?"

Having heard this particular should before, I made my usual response: "You know, Elizabeth Gilbert was an author for many years before she sold the concept of a book based on her postdivorce travels. Traveling and writing for *Eat, Pray, Love* involved self-discovery, but it was her job. If someone offers you a few hundred thousand dollars to see the world, we'll talk."

"That's right," she laughed as she cried. "That was in the book. I forgot about that."

"Why are you asking about this now? Would you like to take a vacation in France?"

Talia broke into deeper sobs. "No, the truth is... I just want to go home."

"Oh. Then let's talk about *that*."

When I asked about the "just" in "just go home," Talia said she felt like going home would be "giving up" or "taking the easy way out." The friends she'd made could not understand why she would want to leave the Bay Area and go back to Tennessee. Her father, someone whose own travels had defined who he was, said this was her chance for adventure. Whenever she hinted she wanted to move home, he would say, "Why would you want to do that?"

Talia's father had settled far away from his own relatives, so Talia grew up in Nashville without grandparents. When holidays rolled around, her childhood friends put on talent shows with their cousins in the backyard and collected dollar bills from Grandma. She and her sisters would have quiet days at home. "It was kind of sad," she said. "I want my kids to know their grandparents."

This time we talked about what was real, not in terms of unemployment rates and starter jobs, but in terms of what was authentic for Talia. I told her that an adult life is built not out of eating, praying, and loving but out of person, place, and thing: who we are with, where we live, and what we do for a living. We start our lives with whichever of these we know something about.

Talia was enjoying her rising career in marketing, and now she had a clear vision about her place. This was encouraging. At a time when many twentysomethings yearn for somewhere to call home and have no idea where they might be in ten years, choosing a place can be incredibly useful. Whether it is moving closer to family or building a life in a city you love, knowing your place is something not to be overlooked.

"Some of my friends are *from* here," Talia said enviously. "They can drive home and have dinner with their parents whenever they want to. I miss my sisters. I wish I could do that. That sounds really nice."

"Why do your sisters get to be in Nashville?"

"Oh, they're the twins. The babies. Well, they've graduated from college now. But they don't care what anybody thinks."

"So they get to be the real rebels and stay home."

"Yeah. Isn't that funny?" Talia laughed ruefully. Then she leaned forward and, in a slightly lowered voice, told me what felt like a secret. "The other day, I was on the bus and I thought to myself: Maybe I've already done it. Maybe this is my big adventure. Maybe this is it."

"Is that scary?" I asked, clearly missing the point. "If this is life's biggest adventure for you?"

With an emphatic, heaving sigh, she nearly shouted, "*No!* It would be a relief! That would mean I could go home."

I sat quietly as Talia cried for a bit. I thought about what I saw when I looked at her. I saw a young woman who had done some exploring, worked hard, and earned some great capital. Now she felt she wasn't allowed to take that home.

Talia's friends invalidated what was real about Talia by assuming that searching was better than finding, friends were better than family, and adventure was better than going home. I couldn't think of a good reason why Talia couldn't go back to Nashville. I asked where this idea had come from.

"My dad. And my friends here."

"Don't your friends want a place to call home?"

"Yeah. But they say I'm too young to talk like this. Like it's too early."

"Too early?" I asked.

"They say, 'Oh, you're cute.' To them, settling down is *settling*. But I go to their apartments, and my neighbor next door, she just sits around and picks apart every guy she dates. And she's still trying to figure out what to do for her career. She's still deciding whether to take the GRE! I look around and... it's... it's just a bunch of furniture that doesn't go together!

And she's in her thirties! I know this sounds mean, but I think... she's not happy at all... and I think... I hope I don't wind up like that."

"What do you want your life to look like when you're in your thirties?"

"I want to be in Nashville, probably working in marketing, maybe as a brand manager. Hopefully I'll have met somebody and we'll have a home. I see myself in Nashville either way."

"So what are you doing here?" I asked.

"Everyone says I should be out in the world exploring. But I *did* that! I just want to go home!" Talia pleaded.

"So you feel some cultural imperative to drag this out."

Talia started to wonder if going back to Nashville was taking the easy way out or if, at this point, she was doing it the hard way. "Why am I going broke living here? Why am I trying to meet someone so far away from where I want to be?" she asked.

"Good questions," I said.

Talia began to look online for jobs in Nashville. She just missed an opening at a marketing firm. "It would have been awesome," she said. "I would love it but the position is closed."

"Call anyway," I said. "It could be closed because they are sitting on a stack of faceless résumés. And find out if you know anybody who knows anybody at that company."

Later that week, Talia called to cancel our session, saying she was on her way to Nashville for an interview. The following week, she walked into my office and said, "I have good news."

Talia enjoyed her last few weeks in town and even felt

nostalgic about her college and postcollege years in California. But when she went next door to tell her thirtysomething neighbor about the new job in Tennessee, the neighbor made a cutting remark about how soon Talia would wind up married with babies. Then she slammed the door in Talia's face and burst into tears behind the door.

Talia tiptoed back to her apartment. She was ready to get on with her life.

The Customized Life

To accept life in its disjointed pieces is an adult experience of freedom, but still these pieces must lodge and embed themselves somewhere, hopefully in a place that allows them to grow and endure.

—Richard Sennett, sociologist

A person's identity is not to be found in behavior... but in the capacity to keep a particular narrative going.

—Anthony Giddens, sociologist

Sessions with Ian did not go smoothly. Like other twentysomethings raised on the promise of doing anything, Ian flinched when faced with the here and now. A life of infinite possibilities had felt like a disorienting and overwhelming burden, but it had also been a liberating fantasy. The concept of "anything" sounded limitless and exciting, while in comparison digital design sounded limiting... and boring.

When we talked about actually moving toward a career in digital design, Ian balked. He did *not* want to "just have some office job and work nine to five like everyone else."

Ian was on a sneaky search for glory. He suffered less from the tyranny of the should than he did from the tyranny of the should-*not*. His life wasn't about getting A's or even the need to realize his potential, at least not in any mainstream way. Conventionality wasn't his niche. Ian's search for glory was the lure of being different, so he displayed what has been called a common symptom of youth: "the dread of doing what has been done before." If he ever chose something to do for work, he didn't want it to be some same-old, everyday thing; his life could be unique.

I didn't completely disagree.

Distinctiveness is a fundamental part of identity. We develop a clearer sense of ourselves by firming up the boundaries between ourselves and others. I am who I am because of how I am different from those around me. There is a point to my life because it cannot be carried out in exactly the same way by any other person. Differentness is part of what makes us who we are. It gives our lives meaning.

But different is simple. Like the easiest way to explain black is to call it the opposite of white, often the first thing we know about ourselves is not what we *are*—it's what we *aren't*. We mark ourselves as not-this or not-that, the way Ian was quick to say he didn't want to sit at the same desk all day. But self-definition cannot end there. An identity or a career cannot be built around what you don't want. We have to shift from a negative identity, or a sense of what I'm not, to a positive one, or a sense of what I am. This takes courage.

A braver form of self-definition dares to be affirmative. Ian needed to move from talking about what he wasn't going to do to talking about what he was going to do. "Being against something is easy," I said. "What are you *for*?"

To Ian, claiming was conforming. By starting a career, he imagined he was agreeing to decades of the status quo. Saying yes to one concrete thing felt like saying no to an interesting or limitless life. In fact, it's the other way around. If Ian didn't say yes to something, his life was going to become unremarkable and limited.

When I sat with Ian, I sometimes thought about a thirty-one-year-old woman I worked with who told me she'd spent her twenties changing her hair color as often as she changed jobs: bright purple when answering phones at a spa, white-blond when temping, deep red when Mystery Shopping, chestnut brown when working in a preschool. When she became engaged, she confided that she planned to quit her latest job. She said, "I can't stand my boss right now. I've got a wedding and a honeymoon to plan, and soon I'll have babies and I'll get to think about something else for a while." When I asked how her fiancé, an elementary school teacher, felt about being the sole breadwinner for a soon-to-be growing family, she shrugged nervously.

And this client made me think of the thirty-nine-year-old female who told me, "At this point in my life, if I'm going to work and pay for child care and be away from my kids all day, I need the work to be interesting and well paid. But I can't get that sort of job. In my twenties, I didn't really deal with what I was going to do about work. In my thirties, I had kids. We need the money and I have to work. But you wouldn't believe the jobs I can't even get. I go for jobs and people just look at me like, 'Why haven't you done something by now?' I wish someone had told me to think about my résumé a long time ago."

Or I thought about the forty-four-year-old male client with a new baby who said to me, "You know, if I'd had a decent psychologist in my twenties, I probably could have started my career before I was thirty-five and had a family before I was in my forties. If you're still doing this in twenty years, I'm sending my son to you." When I asked what he would like me to say to his son, my client replied, "That you can't pull some great career out of a hat in your thirties. You've got to start in your twenties."

With these clients in mind, over the next many months, my sessions with Ian went more or less this way:

I would say, "You need to claim something."

And Ian would say, "But claiming something feels like losing everything else."

Or Ian would say, "I don't want to settle for some ordinary thing."

And I would say, "I'm not talking about settling. I'm talking about starting. Twentysomethings who don't get started wind up with blank résumés and out-of-touch lives only to settle far more down the road. What's so original about that?"

After these conversations, Ian would look at me sideways. Then he'd roll up his pant leg and head out the door toward his bike.

Ian and I needed to come together. The ocean hadn't worked for me. The jar of jam hadn't worked for him. We needed a metaphor we could agree on. After many amicably strained sessions, Ian came rushing in from the bus, venting about waiting for a bike part in the mail. In an ongoing effort to back off, I made small talk. I asked why he couldn't get the part he needed at the cycle shop where he worked. This is when Ian told me he rode a custom bike, and the part he needed had been special-ordered.

I was curious. I knew Ian's bike was his primary mode of transportation, but I also knew he was not a road biker or a mountain biker. I asked why he had a custom bike. He explained he didn't necessarily need one, but he felt this sort of bike was a better reflection of what he wanted to convey to the world.

Now we were on to something.

I asked Ian what a custom bike said about him, compared to a mass-produced one he could buy anywhere, one that might be even easier to maintain. He said the bike represented his feeling that he wanted to be the product of different parts, someone who cannot be defined by a label. Ian's desire for a custom bike was a sincere reflection of what he wanted for himself. He wanted his life to be singular and complex—and great. But the fact that he was looking for a solution at a store said a lot about how his twenties were coming along. Ian had the right idea but found it easier to customize a bike than a life.

In business and culture, we have moved from mass production to mass customization. Progress used to mean turning out the most identical widgets at the least expense for the highest profit. Now we expect to be able to tailor goods and services to suit our wants and needs. Personal computers are self-specified and truly personal. Apps and design-your-own smartphone cases make each phone unique. A custom shirt company encourages consumers to be their own brand. With e-commerce and peer-to-peer marketing we have set aside one-size-fits-all in favor of a "market of one." Companies and marketers have tapped into the innovative life that many, like Ian, want but are not sure how to get: "Let them eat lifestyle!" it is said.

Ian needed to transfer what he knew about building bikes to putting together the pieces of a life. I asked Ian how a custom bike is built. He said he went to a bike store where he was fitted for a frame and wheels. The frame was made based on his measurements and riding needs. Then he specified some other preferences for parts, and received a bike to his liking. As he gradually outfitted his bike, it became more functional and distinctive. This took time and money, but Ian enjoyed the pursuit. The bike represented something important: It was all his own creation.

"So a customized bike fits you," I said.

"Yeah."

"And it's unique," I said.

"Yeah."

"It feels authentic and different. Even limitless in a way, because you can keep changing it over time."

"Yeah, exactly."

"But you started with some standard parts. You didn't literally reinvent the wheel."

"No," he said, smiling. "I didn't."

I asked Ian to consider that maybe that's what an authentic, unique life is. In the twenty-first century, careers and lives don't roll off an assembly line. We have to put together the pieces ourselves. Ian's life could be personalized and changeable, but it was going to take some time and effort—and he would probably need to start with some common parts. Having an uncommon life wasn't going to come from resisting these choices, it was going to come from making these choices. Same as the bike.

Ian could imagine building a life one job or one piece of capital at a time. It seemed less conforming—and less terrifying—than feeling like his next move would decide the one way his life was going to be forever.

"So what are you going to build on?" I asked.

"You mean with work?" Ian asked.

"You need to work. Your life needs to work."

"Different parts of me want to do different things."

"Right. I understand," I said. "So which part do you start with?"

Ian sighed. "I don't know."

"You don't?" I asked. "What about digital design?"

"I've actually been applying for some jobs like that recently," he said sheepishly. "But I'm not even getting interviews. I thought I would sail right through this once I decided what to do. A job in an office isn't looking so bad, especially now that I realize I can't even get one."

I listened while Ian thought.

"I still think about that company in D.C.," he said finally. "You know, the one we talked about with the digital design apprentice program. But I'd never get in. Obviously."

"That doesn't seem obvious to me. Tell me about your application," I said.

After serving on several admissions and hiring committees, I know a fair amount about why one twentysomething is chosen over another for some coveted spot. I have read through hundreds of application packets and seen how numbers fade into the background while artful cover letters and essays stand out in relief. I have watched one applicant get into graduate school at one place while another winds up somewhere else all because of how a fifteen-minute interview felt to the person in charge.

One thing this has taught me is that a good story goes further in the twentysomething years than perhaps at any other time in life. College is done and résumés are fledgling, so the personal narrative is one of the few things currently under our control. As a twentysomething, life is still more about potential than proof. Those who can tell a good story about who they are and what they want leap over those who can't.

Think about the number of applications that hiring managers and graduate programs receive. Countless pieces of paper with lines of capital such as Biology Major, 3.9, University of Tennessee, Piedmont Community College, GMAT 720, Basketball Team, 2.9, Campus Tour Guides, French Minor, Art History Major, University of Washington, Dean's List, GRE 650. Amid the details, a protagonist needs to appear. A good story should take shape. Otherwise, résumés are just lists, and lists are not compelling.

But what is a good story?

If the first step in establishing a professional identity is claiming our interests and talents, then the next step is claiming a story about our interests and talents, a narrative we can take with us to interviews and coffee dates. Whether you are a therapist or an interviewer, a story that balances complexity and cohesion is, frankly, diagnostic. Stories that sound too simple seem inexperienced and lacking. But stories that sound too complicated imply a sort of internal disorganization that employers simply don't want.

I asked Ian what he said about himself when he last applied to the apprenticeship in design. He said he wrote something about staying up all night in high school, putting together the yearbook layout. Ian said the essay was "postmodern and smart" but he had a difficult time explaining it to me. I suggested he try again, that he go for something coherent and smart, something with an obvious narrative arc. Ian resisted this idea, imagining a boring essay that mirrored his résumé. This was a problem because while schools and companies want originality and creativity, they want communication and reasoning even more.

No matter what company or program someone applies to, a sort of game goes on. Interviewers want to hear a reasonable story about the past, present, and future. How does what you did before relate to what you want to do now, and how might that get you to what you want to do next? Everyone realizes most applicants don't actually know what their careers will look like. Even the ones who think they do often change their minds.

As a human resources executive told me, "I don't expect people to say it's their dream to work here forever. I roll my eyes at that. No one knows where they will be in five years. Still, the burden is on the applicants to show that working here makes sense beyond the person just wanting a job or the building being two blocks from their apartment." Life does not need to be linear but it does, as this executive said, need to make sense.

"Ian, you're doing it again," I said. "You're muddling your story because you don't want to commit to anything, much less to anything that makes sense. That makes you sound cagey or chaotic. No one will hire you with a story like that."

"But I don't want to pin myself down," he said.

"To what? Your story isn't a contract. You won't be asked to sign it in blood. It's an introduction."

Reluctantly, Ian created a sharper narrative, one that started with his early interest in drawing. He pulled together his relevant experiences in architecture and cognitive science classes, and a bit about his work. In the opening sentence of the new essay, Ian recalled a time from childhood when he carried around a little spiral flip notebook because he liked to make small abstract pictures for his parents and siblings. His family called him Mr. Logo.

With the same capital and a better story, Ian went to work at the company in D.C. A few years later when he was at another choice point in his life, he wrote this:

> When I made the decision to come to D.C., I worried that by making that choice, I was closing all the other doors open to me at that moment. But it was sort of liberating to make a choice about something. Finally. And, if anything, this job has just opened more doors for me. Now I feel really confident that I will have several iterations of my career—or at least time for several iterations—and that I will be able to do other things in life.
>
> For a long time, it was such a relief to have this job—I felt like I could just live my life and not worry about direction—worries that

> immobilized me in the years after I graduated. Now I am at a point where I don't want to continue in my current position—and I'm pissed! It's hard to think all over again about what the next step is. But it's easier now because I know from experience that I have to take action, that debating isn't going to get me anywhere.
>
> Sometimes making choices feels like planning for my life in a way that seems boring. Sometimes making choices to pursue things that seem like good fits, or that match my interests, seems boring simply because it makes sense. I find myself wanting to go off in an unexpected direction—Arabic! Cambodia! I know this is a sort of crazy impulse. I know that the way to live a good life is to pursue things that are not only interesting to you but that make sense.
>
> Above all else in my life, I feared being ordinary. Now I guess you could say I had a revelation of the day-to-day. I finally got it there's a reason everybody in the world lives this way—or at least starts out this way—because this is how it's done.

Ian was right. This is how it's done. This is how it starts. Claiming a career or getting a good job isn't the end; it's the beginning. And, then, there is still a lot more to know and a lot more to do.

LOVE

An Upmarket Conversation

[Society] is structured to distract people from the decisions that have a huge impact on happiness in order to focus attention on the decisions that have a marginal impact on happiness. The most important decision any of us make is who we marry. Yet there are no courses on how to choose a spouse.

—David Brooks, political and cultural commentator

In 2009, David Brooks, a columnist for the *New York Times*, wrote an article about being asked to give a commencement speech. In the piece, he said he had writer's block. He felt he wasn't supposed to say what he really wanted to say, which was something about how happiness has more to do with whom you marry than with what college you attend. He opined that while universities offer countless classes on semiotics, there is not a single course on being smart about marriage, and that this is "the chief way our society is messed up." Brooks aptly observed that we have to go downmarket, to talk shows or reality shows, to hear marriage discussed at all.

I don't know if Mr. Brooks talked about getting married when he gave the commencement address, but I can imagine the horror and alienation among the graduates if he had. I can see hundreds of baccalaureates standing there in cap and gown, mouths agape, wondering what exactly marriage had to do with them.

At that moment, probably very little.

Today's twentysomethings spend more time single than any generation in history. Most will spend years on their own, somewhere between their childhood homes and families of their own. This time gives many people a chance to live it up before they settle down, and to have fun with friends and lovers while the options are open. Some people find each other through friends while others connect online or around town. Some are serial monogamists while others pair with as many people as they can. Pundits and parents worry that marriage is dead, dating is in demise, and hooking up is the new relational medium.

But the moratorium on marriage is relative. Young Americans do marry later than their parents did—on average about five years later—and this statistic especially holds in urban areas. Currently, the average age for first marriage is twenty-six for women and twenty-eight for men, with more than half of adults marrying over the age of twenty-five.

But the United States is still the most marrying nation in the Western world. About 50 percent of Americans marry by age thirty, 75 percent by the age of thirty-five, and 85 percent by the age of forty. Even though marriage may seem almost irrelevant, most twentysomethings—male or female, gay or straight—will be married or partnered or dating their future partner within about ten years' time.

As passé or postponed as marriage or partnership may seem, what is even less in vogue is talking about it. Popular magazines portray a twentysomething culture dominated by singles who are almost obsessed with avoiding commitment. But behind closed doors, I hear a different story. I have yet to meet a twentysomething who doesn't want to get married or at least find a committed relationship. The clients with fast-paced lives or high-profile jobs just feel compelled to whisper about it and hope for the best. It seems too conventional, or at least politically incorrect, to be strategic about such things. Even clients who desperately want to be married seem embarrassed, or even superstitious, about staking claim to any particular relational dream. We seem to believe that relationships are completely out of our control.

Career, on the other hand, is what we can plan for. Specificity of professional desire is admired among many, and we spend years gaining mastery over our work lives. Guidance counselors help us plot our high school trajectories. Educational consultants charge as much as $30,000 to help kids prepare college applications. Test-prep companies offer courses, and private tutors, for college or graduate entrance exams. Major advisers help us figure out what path to take in college and graduate school. Internship-placement services can cost thousands of dollars. Business degrees guarantee access to network databases. Doctoral-level degrees ensure expertise.

As we build a career, it seems there is a book, class, degree, consultant, or service available at every turn. Maybe that's as it should be, because careers are important. But along the way, because of these very choice points, there is so much room for revision that developing your career in no way compares to choosing a partner or spouse. Maybe this was what David Brooks meant when he said that whom you marry is the most important decision in your life.

Marriage is one of our most defining moments because so much is wrapped up in it. If building a career is like spending twelve hours at the blackjack table—seeing the cards as you make your decisions, playing each hand with current winnings in mind, having a new opportunity to take a chance or play it safe with every card dealt—then choosing a mate is like walking over to the roulette wheel and putting all your chips on red 32. With one decision you choose your partner in all adult things. Money, work, lifestyle, family, health, leisure, retirement, and even death become a three-legged race. Almost every aspect of your life will be intertwined with almost every aspect of your partner's life. And let's face it, if things don't work out, a marriage cannot just be left off a résumé like a failed job. Even as a divorced couple, you may be forever tied, financially and logistically, as you pay for schools and meet every other weekend in the driveway to exchange the kids.

Most twentysomethings are painfully aware of the significance of marriage. If "remarriage is the triumph of hope over experience," then, as researcher Jeffrey Arnett observes, even a first marriage for many twentysomethings is a victory. Half of today's twentysomethings have been left in the wake of divorce, and all know someone who was.

In the twentieth century, it was tempting to minimize the effects of divorce. Some adults in unhappy marriages imagined trickle-down happiness: They would be happier after divorce; therefore, so would their kids. But as these kids matured, "the unexpected legacy of divorce" was undeniable. Many children of divorce said they had not much noticed—or cared—whether their parents were happily married. What they did know was that their lives fell apart after their parents split, as resources and parents became stretched too thin. So while we hear a lot about twentysomethings who just want to have fun before marriage, many are also waiting to commit in hopes of being luckier in love than their parents were.

But doing something later is not necessarily the same as doing something better. This may explain why, even as the average age of marriage rises, the divorce rate holds steady at about 40 percent. More and more twentysomethings are careful not to rush into marriage at a young age, yet many do not know what else to consider. The timeline has changed, but a new conversation has not yet begun.

One of the first big research projects I worked on as a graduate student was a study that followed about a hundred women from their twenties into their seventies. At midlife, each woman was asked to write one page about her most difficult life experience so far. Some stories were about tough bosses or unrequited love. A few were about tragic illnesses. But many of the saddest, most protracted stories were about bad marriages. Some had ended in divorce and others were continuing on.

The women in this study were twenty-one in the early 1960s, and 80 percent of them were married by twenty-five. When I worked on this research, I was in my late twenties and unmarried. I remember feeling relieved that my generation had the luxury of marrying later. I was sure that my cohort and those who followed would have happier marriages because we got to explore before we settled down. Now I know that postponing marriage, in and of itself, does not make for a better union.

The trend toward later marriages is a relatively new one, so scientists are only beginning to measure and understand what it means for couples. It is well established that teen marriages are the most unstable of all unions and this, coupled with what we now know about the maturation that goes on in one's twenties, has led many to believe that when it comes to marriage, the later the better. This is not exactly what researchers are finding.

The most recent studies show that marrying later than the teen years does indeed protect against divorce, but this only holds true until about age twenty-five. After twenty-five, one's age at marriage does not predict divorce. These findings run counter to the notion that it is unquestionably better to postpone marriage as long as you can.

Older spouses may be more mature, but later marriage has its own challenges. Rather than growing together while their twentysomething selves are still forming, partners who marry older may be more set in their ways. And a series of low-commitment, possibly destructive relationships can create bad habits and erode faith in love. And even though searching may help you find a better partner, the pool of available singles shallows over time, perhaps in more ways than one.

These are all real considerations, but the challenge I hear about most in my practice is related to what has been termed the Age Thirty Deadline. The Age Thirty Deadline is the quiet but nagging concern that so many twentysomethings have. What to do about relationships in our twenties may not be clear—or even seem imminently important—but "I'd better not be alone at thirty" is a common refrain.

At thirty, this nagging concern crawls out of its corner and becomes full-blown panic. The exact timing and pitch of the age pressure varies, depending on where someone lives and what their peers are doing. And women can feel more stress around this than men because they may have less time to start a family, and they may feel they have less power as they imagine sitting around waiting for a ring.

In my experience, the Age Thirty Deadline is more of an Age Thirty Bait and Switch. Everything that was OK at twenty-nine suddenly feels awful and, in an instant, we feel behind. Almost overnight, commitment changes from being something for later to being something for yesterday. Marriage goes from being something we'll worry about at thirty to being something we want at thirty. When, then, is the time to really *think* about partnership? This sudden shift can lead to all kinds of trouble.

Let's compare the sorts of things I hear from those in their twenties and thirties. This is what twentysomethings say:

> I don't think a lot about who I date. If the person is fun to talk to and there's good sex, that's enough. What more is there to worry about? I'm only twenty-seven.

> I love my girlfriend. We've been together three years. But I'm not planning on factoring

her in to where I go to graduate school. I'm just not supposed to be thinking about this in my mid-twenties. I imagined this would all come a lot later.

I want to get married by twenty-eight and have my first child by thirty-one, but I feel silly when I say that to people. There's this stigma that you can't really plan for that kind of stuff. It feels like I'm fourteen again and playing pretend house. My boyfriend tells me he wants to own a home by the age of thirty-five. During another conversation, I told him I want to have my first baby when I'm thirty to thirty-two. He told me it's not realistic to decide when to have a baby, that's going to depend on where we are in our careers, how much money we have, where we live. So how can he say he plans to buy a home by a certain age? It's like a double standard. And it seems like it's easier and more realistic to plan our careers and financial stability than to plan our marriages and babies.

My boyfriend and I got together because we were both heading west. We moved in together when we got here because it was easier. We both like kayaking and all that but we're not serious. I'd never marry him.

I love my boyfriend and, I can only say this to you, I want to marry him. But I feel like I'm not allowed to want that at this point in my life. So we keep taking these breaks to date other people and then we end up talking all the time and getting back together. It's like neither one of us thinks we can say you're it. Like there is something wrong with that.

So many of my twentysomething clients either don't take their relationships seriously or don't think they are allowed to. Then somewhere around thirty, getting married suddenly seems pressing. Now listen in on my thirtysomething clients, some of whom are only a year or two older than the clients we just heard from:

> Every time somebody on Facebook changes their status to engaged or married, I panic. I'm convinced Facebook was invented to make single people feel bad about their lives.

> My dad always says, "Don't turn out like Aunt Betty." She's single.

> Whenever my boyfriend goes out of town and we don't see each other for a weekend—or, God forbid, a week—I think that's just one week later until we get engaged. I want to lock this thing down now.

> I'm not gonna be that balding guy at the bars whose friends have all moved on.

> My boyfriend put a ring box under the Christmas tree last year. It wasn't an engagement ring. I'm still mad about it.

> Friday and Saturday nights are all right until all the couples start getting their coats. I try to leave before that happens because it feels crappy, being one of the leftover people.

> Next week is my birthday and I don't even want to celebrate it. It might get my boyfriend thinking about whether I have old eggs.

> Anything I do where I'm not meeting my husband is a total waste of time.

> The best boyfriend I ever had was when I was in my midtwenties. I just didn't think I was supposed to be with someone then. Now I feel like I missed the ones who were willing to settle down and I'm scrambling to marry whoever I can.

This client perhaps best summarizes the dangers that surround the Age Thirty Bait and Switch:

> Dating for me in my twenties was like this musical-chairs thing. Everybody was running around and having fun. Then I hit thirty and it was like the music stopped and everybody started sitting down. I didn't want to be the only one left without a chair. Sometimes I think

> I married my husband just because he was the closest chair to me at thirty. Sometimes I think I should have just waited for someone who might be a better partner, and maybe I should have, but that seemed risky. What I really wish I'd done is thought more about marriage sooner. Like when I was in my twenties.

These chapters aren't about whether thirtysomethings should sit down in the closest chair or whether they should keep looking, whether thirtysomethings should settle or be picky. Those articles and books have been written. That debate is raging on.

The chapters ahead are about twentysomething men and women *not* settling—not settling for spending their twenties on no-criteria or low-criteria relationships that likely have little hope or intention of succeeding. These chapters are about *not* waiting to get picky until you are in your thirties and the save-the-dates start pouring in. They are about being choosy about the right things when you can still think clearly about claiming your life. Besides, like with work, good relationships don't just appear when we're ready. It may take a few thoughtful tries before we know what love and commitment really are.

Around the time I was a twentysomething doing research on the stories about difficult marriages, I saw my first psychotherapy client, a twenty-six-year-old named Alex. When Alex was assigned to me, I felt relieved. I hadn't been a graduate student long enough to be an expert in anything, but the twenties I thought I could handle. Alex didn't meet the criteria for any disorder and, with the funny stories she brought to her sessions, it was easy for me to nod my head while we kicked the can down the road. But it was my job to take Alex's twentysomething life seriously. I just didn't know it yet.

My supervisor informed me that the nodding therapists we see on television are stereotypes, and that if I wanted to be helpful, I needed to be less patient. This was good news because I am an impatient person. But I didn't know what to be less patient about. Hadn't my supervisor heard? Work happened later, marriage happened later, kids happened later, even death happened later. Twentysomethings like Alex and me had nothing but time.

To me, Alex's twenties seemed difficult but kind of, well, trivial. The way I saw it, her real life hadn't started yet. She was job-hopping and hooking up with men. She wasn't raising kids or preparing for tenure. When my supervisor pushed me to take up Alex's current relationship, I protested: "Sure, she's dating down, but it's not like she's marrying the guy." Then my supervisor said, "Not yet. But she might marry the next one. Regardless, the best time to work on Alex's marriage is before she has one."

She had me there.

Picking Your Family

Other things may change us, but we start and end with family.
—Anthony Brandt, writer

In the world of mental health, the lowest-functioning clients and the highest-functioning clients receive the worst care. The lowest-functioning clients typically struggle with serious mental illnesses that are maintained more than cured. And, because of downward drift that draws a disproportionate number of such patients into the lower income brackets, these clients often do not have access to top-notch care. The highest-functioning clients, on the other hand, usually have a lot going for them, including family or schools that connect them with private therapists when needed.

These high-functioning clients are what therapists call YAVIS—young, attractive, verbal, intelligent, and successful—and these qualities bestow all sorts of social and psychological advantages. Being young means, as a colleague once put it, "that you haven't completely screwed up your life yet." Being verbal allows you to easily exchange a common currency with friends and bosses as you parlay being talkative into social status. Intelligence aids achievement and problem-solving, and even leadership. Successful people are generally brimming with confidence. And, as Aristotle said, "beauty is a greater recommendation than any letter of introduction." So, YAVIS clients are well received nearly everywhere they go, and many therapists light up when one comes walking in the door.

Still, there are two paths to being smart and charming when you are young: Life has been good or life has been bad. When life has been good, maybe someone goes to see a therapist for a while because some isolated thing is not currently going well. Most likely, the difficulty will be resolved quickly and the client will be on his way.

When life has been bad, someone goes to see a therapist because even though things look pretty on the outside the person feels horrible on the inside, and this is a discrepancy that even many therapists cannot hold. Sometimes it is just too jarring to imagine that someone who seems so perfect has lived a life that has been so imperfect. What results is a therapy where the client's image gets in the way of the help that he or she needs. The client has come to focus on what has not gone well, but the therapist is blinded by what has. Too often, being successful when you are young is about survival. Some people are good at hiding their troubles. They are good at "falling up."

Emma was one of these people. She grew up in a family perched on the fragile edge of the middle class. Early childhood went well enough but then, as happens in more families than you might imagine, things quickly declined. Her father ran up credit card debt. Her mother's social drinking turned into alcoholism. Her father lost his job and turned to suicide. Emma moved through school and friends like nothing had changed, but her interior was infused with sadness.

I liked Emma immediately, which is not surprising since resilient people are usually very likeable. For years, she had been presenting herself as a vanilla twentysomething. She had been spoon-feeding the world these subtly pleasing tastes of herself. She got along with everybody. She was good at most things. She went with everything. Her early therapy sessions were equally as palatable. She came on time and often began the hour by asking how I was.

One day, Emma mixed up the time of her session, arriving an hour early. I had an appointment with another client, so Emma had to stay in the waiting room until it was her turn. When she came into my office, she nervously said, "I'm camping out in your waiting room. You must think I've got some serious problems." I smiled and said, "You tell me."

Emma slumped over in her chair and broke into tears. When she raised her head she was ready to talk. She said, "I feel like the loneliest person in the whole world." I liked her even more after that.

Emma had fallen so far up that she felt she lived the life of an imposter. She excelled at her top-tier school but felt like an outsider who didn't belong. Her family life was nothing like what everyone else described about their own, so she kept any real details about herself to herself. Only in my office did her past and her present collide and, for a couple of years, I listened to what Emma had been through—and what she was still going through. Emma graduated with honors and, when other kids' families swooped into town with bouquets of flowers and dinner reservations, she skipped the ceremonies and left the state for a good job. I was happy and sad for her at the same time.

A couple of years later, Emma moved back to her old college town, and we continued our work together. She now faced what it was like to be a nearly orphaned twentysomething who still had a lot of life ahead. She was exhausted, but she had some good friends. "You can't pick your family, but you can pick your friends," she said cheerfully yet unconvincingly.

Emma's friends were very kind. "I'm here for you!" and "You can be part of my family!" they chimed. But as only a child without a family of her own knows, it's not the same. Friends can do long talks and good cries, but at holiday time or very hard times everyone teamed up with family, and Emma was left standing alone.

One day she hung her head in her lap and sobbed most of the hour. She had just bought a new address book, and she came undone as she filled in her many contacts but stared at the empty "In Case of Emergency, Please Call" blank. She was almost hysterical when she looked at me and said, "Who's gonna be there for me if I have a car wreck? Who's gonna help me if I get cancer?"

It took every bit of professional restraint I had not to say, "I will!" But that would have been about making myself feel better. Instead, I gave her my sincere attention and said, "We need to get you a new family."

In her midtwenties by this point, Emma had been dating

the same man for almost a year. I knew a lot about her career but not much about him. I'd hear "it's fine," "he's fun," "we have a good time." For a young woman who felt so alone, this seemed a woefully inadequate relationship, or at least a woefully inadequate description, so I pressed for more.

I found out her boyfriend didn't talk a lot. He watched a lot of TV and hated working. He could be jealous and would scream at her. I didn't like what I heard at all, and I told Emma so.

"How can you be so ambitious about work but so unambitious about relationships?" I asked.

"I have to have a really good job to survive," she said. "But a really good relationship is more than I can hope for. It's more than I can do anything about anyway."

"No, it's not," I said.

Often the clients with the toughest family backgrounds know the least about how to get what they want in love. But these are the clients who need to be the most careful. They are the very clients who need to partner well.

Emma came to my office one Monday. She'd spent the weekend meeting her boyfriend's parents for the first time. Both nights she cried into her pillow and missed her previous boyfriend. This surprised me, because Emma and her former boyfriend had mostly made each other miserable. But I also remembered she had loved his family a great deal. They spent wonderful holidays together and enjoyed the little things like movies and dinners and reading the paper.

I asked for more details about what it was like to be with her current boyfriend's family. The father was an astronomer who spent most of the time outside on his telescope, while the mother watched TV. Neither parent was particularly interested in their son or Emma. This gave me pause.

"Emma, you say you can't pick your family but you can pick your friends. That was true growing up. Now you're about to pick your family, and I'm concerned you're not making a good choice."

Emma's eyes welled up with tears and she stared out my office window. "I can't expect my boyfriend's parents to be perfect. Mine aren't."

"You're right. No family is perfect. But your tears after meeting these parents, I think they are telling us something."

"Yeah. I'm not psyched about my boyfriend's family."

"You can keep learning to live with the fact that family will never envelop you. Maybe creating that for your own children will be enough. But it is hard work, spending a lifetime giving something you never get. When you partner with someone, you have a second chance at family."

Emma started to have an ambition for her family. She dreamed of a caring and capable husband and two or three kids. She even allowed herself to envision in-laws who would be loving and involved grandparents. She hoped for beach vacations with three generations digging in the sand.

Emma had the define-the-relationship talk with her boyfriend. At thirty, he wasn't sure he would ever want children. And he imagined spending as little time as possible with his extended family or anyone else's. He didn't want family to get in the way of the things he still wanted to do.

Emma ended their relationship. She laughed it off, saying her life had become an *Onion* headline she had seen: "Weekend with Boyfriend's Parents Explains a Lot." I knew she was scared.

There *is* something scary about picking your family. It's not romantic. It means you aren't just waiting for your soulmate to arrive. It means you know you are making decisions that will affect the rest of your life. It means you are thinking about the fact that your relationship needs to work not only in the here and now but also in the there and then.

Twentysomethings who aren't at least a little scared about their relationships are often the ones who are being the least thoughtful. I wasn't exactly glad Emma was scared, but I knew her fear was useful. It meant she was taking love as seriously as she had always taken work.

When people meet my two children for the first time, they sometimes say, "King's choice!" This is because I happened to have a boy and a girl and so, if I were a king, I would have a son to carry on the empire and a daughter to marry off to a neighboring country where I hoped to gain favor. It is strange to have that image invoked about two twenty-first-century children who will likely grow up and lead their lives as they choose. Plus, I bristle a little at the thought of my daughter's wedding being a business deal. But the expression also reminds me that, for many centuries, marriage was about bridging families.

Today, we see marriage as a commitment between two individuals. Western culture is generally individualistic, prizing independence and self-fulfillment in almost all areas. We emphasize rights over duties and choice over obligation. This extends especially to marriage. With some notable exceptions, there has never been more freedom to decide whether, when, and how to partner, and with whom. There is no question that this has led to countless happy unions, as well as the experience of owning one of the most important decisions of our lives. At the same time, the foregrounding of the individual in relationships has caused us to forget about one of our greatest twentysomething opportunities: picking and creating our families.

Clients like Emma feel destined for unhappiness because of broken families. They grew up believing that family was beyond their control, or something other people got to have. The only solution they have ever known has been to turn to friends or therapists or boyfriends for moments of solace, or to swear off family altogether. What no one tells twentysomethings like Emma is that finally, and suddenly, they can pick their own families—they can create their own families—and *these* are the families that life will be about. *These* are the families that will define the decades ahead.

Emma left town for a bigger city and another good job. She got serious about family. She set her mind to making for herself what had been missing all her life. About three years later, Emma married someone who gave her that second chance at family. She and her husband sound happy together and are enjoying the one young child they have so far. Emma writes that her in-laws bought an apartment in their town so they could help with the grandkids and be a regular part of their lives. Her two sisters-in-law live nearby, and have been there for fun dinners and beach vacations.

Now, she notices, emergency-contact blanks don't seem big enough.

The Cohabitation Effect

Making the best of things is a damn poor way of dealing with them. My life has been a series of escapes from that quicksand.
—Rose Wilder Lane, writer

At thirty-two, Jennifer's parents threw her a lavish wine-country wedding, complete with pink tulips and great music. By then, Jennifer and Carter had lived together more than three years. The event was attended by their friends, families, and two dogs.

When Jennifer started therapy with me about six months later, she was finishing her thank-you notes and looking for a divorce lawyer. Carter was already couch-surfing elsewhere, so it was a matter of days until everyone heard about the split. Jennifer said she felt like a fraud. "I spent more time planning the wedding than I spent happily married," she sobbed.

Jennifer always looked halfway between a business meeting and a hangover. She dressed smartly but often seemed tired and disheveled. She had gone to a top-ten school and was starting to have the career in public relations to prove it, but she also still partied with relative abandon.

Carter was a job-hopper without a professional identity. Rather than completing his last year of college, he'd gone on tour with his bluegrass band. The band fizzled, but his love for music continued. He worked here and there as a sound engineer and band promoter. Jennifer and Carter were, perhaps, the coolest, hippest couple in their crowd. They loved talking about what shows to see next.

After the wedding, conversations changed. A real-estate agent sat them down for mortgage calculations. Factoring in a baby made their financial outlook worse. Jennifer hoped to work part-time while her kids were small, so soon she would need Carter to earn much more money. She started to think about living back in New Hampshire, where things would be cheaper and her parents could help. Carter wanted to stay where they were, maybe for good. Their fun-filled life became a somber stalemate.

What was most disheartening to Jennifer was she felt she'd tried to do everything right. "My parents got married young. They dated for, like, six months and I know my mom never even had sex before she got married. How were they supposed to know if it was going to work? Carter and I were older. We lived together for, like, three years. How did this happen?" she cried into a tissue.

In psychotherapy, there's a saying that "the slower you go, the faster you get there." Sometimes the best way to help people is to slow them down long enough to examine their own thinking. Everyone has gaps in their reasoning. If you stop and shine a light on these mental ellipses, you find assumptions that drive behavior without our being aware of them. As Jennifer spoke, one assumption was easy to spot: Living together is a good test for marriage. This is a common misperception.

Cohabitation in the United States has increased more than 1,500 percent in the past fifty years. In 1960, about 500,000 unmarried couples lived together. Now, the number is almost 8,000,000. About half of twentysomethings will live with a romantic partner at least once during their twenty-something years. More than half of all marriages will be preceded by cohabitation. This shift has largely been attributed to the sexual revolution and the availability of birth control, and certainly the economics of young adulthood play a role. But when you talk to twentysomethings themselves, you hear about something else: cohabitation as prophylaxis.

In a representative nationwide survey, nearly half of twentysomethings agreed with the statement "You would only marry someone if he or she agreed to live together with you first, so that you could find out whether you really got along." About two-thirds of twentysomethings believe that moving in together before marriage is a good way to avoid divorce.

Jennifer was in this group. She imagined that, unlike her own divorced parents who married young and fast, she would be more successful if she waited to get married and if she lived with her partner first. But couples who "live together first" are actually *less* satisfied with their marriages and *more* likely to divorce than couples who do not. This is what sociologists call the cohabitation effect.

The cohabitation effect has baffled many marital researchers. Some have fallen back on the explanation that those who cohabitate may be less conventional and more open to divorce in the first place. But research shows that the cohabitation effect is not fully explained by individual characteristics such as religion, education, or politics. Similarly, in my private practice it is not the case that liberals cohabitate and conservatives do not. In fact, the trend toward cohabitation is continuing in both red and blue states—just as it has in every other Western nation.

So what accounts for the cohabitation effect? Why are couples who cohabitate more likely to wind up divorced? The latest research suggests it is something about cohabitation itself.

Sliding, Not Deciding

Jennifer and I worked to answer her question of "How did this happen?"

Over many sessions, we talked about how she and Carter went from dating to living together. Consistent with studies that report most couples say it "just happened," Jennifer said, "It was just easier. We were paying two rents and sleeping over at each other's places a lot. I was always leaving something I needed for work at one apartment or another. We liked to be together a lot, so it was just cheaper and more convenient. Living together was a quick decision, but if it didn't work out there was a quick exit."

Jennifer was talking about what is known as "sliding, not deciding." Moving from dating to sleeping over to sleeping over a lot to cohabitation can be a gradual slope, one not marked by rings or ceremonies or sometimes even a conversation. Couples often bypass talking about why they want to live together and what it will mean.

When researchers ask twentysomethings these questions, women are more likely to say they want better access to love, while men say they want easier access to sex. It is not uncommon for two partners to have different, unspoken—even unconscious—agendas for cohabitation. But both men and women agree that their standards for a live-in partner are lower than for a spouse.

I asked Jennifer if she slid into living with Carter, if she was less intentional about moving in together than she would have been about engagement or marriage.

"That was the point," she said. "It *wasn't* marriage, so thinking it through wasn't supposed to matter."

"What if you think about it now?"

"I think my criteria were good sex, fun weekends, cool crowd, cheaper rent."

"Did you have concerns about moving in together?"

"Rattling around in the back of my head there were thoughts about Carter not having any real career in the works. I think I thought living together would be a good way to test out how serious he was going to get about things. Except now I can see we never actually treated living together very seriously. The fact that he worked in music made him the perfect twentysomething boyfriend. His life was built around having a good time. Our lives were built around having a good time."

Like many twentysomethings who cohabitate, Jennifer and Carter's life together sounded more like an intersection between college roommate and sex partner than a lifelong commitment between two spouses. They vaguely had the idea of testing their relationship, but they didn't venture into areas that typically stress a marriage: They didn't pay a mortgage, try to get pregnant, get up in the night with kids, spend holidays with in-laws when they didn't want to, save for college and retirement, or see each other's paychecks and credit-card bills. Living with someone may have benefits, but approximating marriage is not necessarily one of them. This is *especially* true at a time when the twentysomething years are touted as a chance to have fun.

"Then what happened?" I asked.

"A year or two into it, I started wondering what we were doing."

"A year? Or two? Which was it?" I queried.

"I don't know..." Jennifer replied.

"So time was sliding also," I said.

"Oh, absolutely. Everything about it was fuzzy. That fuzziness ended up being the most frustrating part. I felt like I was on this multiyear, never-ending audition to be his wife. That made me really insecure. There was a lot of game-playing and arguing. I never felt like he was really committed to me. I still don't, obviously."

Jennifer's fears were perhaps well founded. To understand why, it helps to know that the cohabitation effect is technically a pre-engagement cohabitation effect, not a premarital cohabitation effect. Couples who live together before marriage but *after becoming engaged,* who combine their lives after making a clear and public commitment, are not any more likely to have distressed or dissolved marriages than couples who do not cohabitate before marriage. They do not suffer from the cohabitation effect.

It is the couples who live together *before an engagement* who are more likely to experience poorer communication, lower levels of commitment to the relationship, and greater marital instability down the road. Multiple studies have shown that those who live with their partners before an engagement are less dedicated before, and even after, marriage. This has been found to be especially true for men. A life built on top of a "Maybe We Will" simply may not feel as consciously committed as a life built on top of the "I Do" of marriage or the "We Are" of engagement.

Jennifer and I started to talk about how she and Carter moved from cohabitation to marriage, a transition so full of choices and rituals it could not possibly have "just happened."

"Marriage did *not* just happen," Jennifer said, rolling her eyes. "I had to kick Carter's butt around the block about the ring, the date, the venue, the invitations. Everything."

"Why did you work so hard?"

"He hadn't turned into husband material, but our lives weren't set up for us to act like adults. I sort of assumed it would come together once we were married."

"You assumed that."

"I hoped it." Jennifer chuckled grimly. "I also thought, 'What other choice do I have?' "

"You could have ended it."

"That didn't feel so easy."

"So much for the quick exit you mentioned," I said.

"It was more like quicksand," Jennifer said gloomily.

Lock-In

Jennifer's reference to quicksand didn't surprise me. Sliding into cohabitation wouldn't be a problem if sliding out were as easy. It isn't.

Too often, twentysomethings enter into what they imagine will be low-cost, low-risk living situations only to find themselves unable to get out months or years later. It's like signing up for a credit card with 0 percent interest for the first year. At the end of twelve months, when the interest goes up to 23 percent, you feel stuck because your balance is too high to pay off and you didn't get around to transferring your balance to another low-interest card sooner. In fact, cohabitation can be exactly like that. In behavioral economics, it's known as consumer lock-in.

Lock-in is the decreased likelihood to search for other options, or change to another option, once an investment in something has been made. The initial investment, called a setup cost, can be big or small. A form. An entrance fee. The hassle of creating an online account. A down payment on a car. The greater the setup costs, the less likely we are to move to another, even better, situation later. But even a minimal investment can lead to lock-in, especially when we are faced with switching costs.

Switching costs—or the time, money, or effort it requires to make a change—are more complex. When we make an initial investment in something, switching costs are hypothetical and in the future, so we tend to underestimate them. It is easy to imagine we'll just get a new credit card later or deal with breaking a lease when the time comes. The problem is when the time does come, the switching costs seem bigger up close than they did from far away.

Cohabitation is loaded with setup and switching costs, the basic ingredients of lock-in. Moving in together can be fun and economical, and the setup costs are subtly woven in. After years living among a roommate's junky old stuff, we happily split the rent on a nice one-bedroom apartment. Couples share Wi-Fi and pets and enjoy shopping for new furniture together. Later, these setup costs have an effect on how likely we are to leave.

"We had all this furniture," Jennifer said. "We had our dogs and all the same friends. We had a weekend routine. It just made it really, really difficult to break up."

When I explained lock-in to Jennifer, she swallowed hard. "When I was a teenager, I gave my mom such a bad time about staying with my dad as long as she did when she obviously wasn't happy. I understand her a lot more now. It's not easy to get out of a live-in relationship. And she had two kids to think about. I stayed with Carter because I couldn't afford to get a new couch," Jennifer cried remorsefully.

"Getting a new couch *can* feel like an insurmountable obstacle to a twentysomething"—I said as Jennifer wept some more—"but I'm guessing it was more than the couch. What other switching costs were there?"

Jennifer thought for a while and said, "My age changed all the switching costs. When we moved in together, I was in my twenties. It seemed like it would be easy to move out if I wanted to. But when I turned thirty, everything felt different."

"The switching costs of starting over after thirty felt greater," I said.

"Everybody was getting married. *I* wanted to get married. Then it was like Carter and I got married because we were living together once we got into our thirties."

"Getting married sooner started to feel more important than whether it would work later," I said.

"I'm really, really embarrassed to admit this, but I almost

didn't care whether it was going to work out. I thought even if it didn't work out, at least I would have gotten married when everybody else was. I would have been on track." Jennifer sniffled.

"So you underestimated the switching costs first of cohabitation and then of marriage."

"Definitely. Getting divorced has been a lot worse than I thought it would be. I don't necessarily regret being with Carter, but I do wish I'd never lived with him, or maybe that I'd been more willing to leave before everything went this far. Now I'm starting over anyway. In a much worse way."

"But you *are* getting out of lock-in," I reminded her. "How are you doing it?"

"I had to face facts. Carter was a great twentysomething boyfriend, but he's no thirtysomething husband and he's never going to be. I'm ready to grow up. My job is going well and I want to have a family. Carter isn't ready for any of that. I don't know if he ever will be, or if he will be in a time frame that makes any sense for me. Somehow, that wasn't real, or official, until we officially got married. Then the excitement of the wedding was behind me. The reality of our future was all that was left. The future wasn't the future anymore. It was now."

Jennifer isn't the only client I've had who's regretted moving in with someone. Some wish they hadn't sunk years into relationships that would have only lasted months had they not been living together. Others are twentysomethings or thirtysomethings who mostly feel, or who want to feel, committed to their relationships, yet they are also confused about whether they have consciously chosen their mate. Founding a relationship on convenience and ambiguity can interfere with the process of claiming the people we love. We all ought to feel confident we are choosing our partners and our partners are choosing us because we want to be with them, not because staying together is convenient or because breaking up is inconvenient.

Cohabitating couples can break up and are a bit more likely to split than married couples. But many cohabitating couples, like Jennifer and Carter, don't break up. They slide from dating to cohabitation. Then they lock into marriage because getting married seems easier than dividing up the furniture and starting over, especially when friends start walking down the aisle. The more aware singles are of this, the more they can understand what living together is... and what it isn't. I am not for or against living together, but I am for twentysomethings knowing that, far from safeguarding against divorce, moving in with someone increases your chances of locking in on someone, whether he or she is right for you or not.

There are things you can do to lessen the cohabitation effect. One is, obviously, don't cohabitate before an engagement. Since this is not an entirely realistic suggestion, researchers also recommend getting clear on each person's commitment level before you move in, and anticipating and regularly evaluating those constraints that may keep you from leaving even if you want to. There are also other ways to test a relationship besides moving in, including doing a wider variety of activities together than dating and sex. There are other ways to figure out whether you and your partner are in love, or even in like.

On Dating Down

Conversation is to be thought of as creating a social world just as causality generates a physical one.

—Rom Harré, psychologist

When Cathy was a teenager, each time she left the house she did so underneath her mother's disapproving glare. Her mother said she needed a different outfit or a better body. Her father told her she was "too much," "too loud"—too *something.* After what felt like nightly fights with her parents, Cathy fell asleep on her bedroom floor with her iPod on and her earbuds in. The next morning she'd wake up in time to be packed off to school, where things were no more forgiving.

Cathy's mother was Korean and her father was white, and they preferred not to discuss race. They raised her not to "see color" and praised living in a "postracial society." But society—and school—were not postracial for Cathy. Cathy went through high school pegged as a cultural stereotype, despite the fact she was nothing like the quiet student people assumed she was. At Cathy's Southern university, where the standard of beauty was blond and smiley, she hardly felt noticed at all.

Now a cheery elementary-school teacher, Cathy "dated down" to an extreme. During the day, she was a dedicated professional who had published one novella for young readers and was working on a second. In the evenings, she lived a somewhat different life. She never chose her boyfriends or sex partners; she let them choose her. She became involved with almost any man who showed interest. She sometimes had unprotected sex. She often responded to the two-a.m. booty text, accepting even the thinnest excuses about why the person did not text earlier. Her attitude about any man who came along was "This could work."

When I expressed concern over Cathy's interactions with men, she dismissed me by saying, "It's just practice. The twenties are a dress rehearsal."

"And look at what you're practicing," I said. "Consider what part you're rehearsing to play."

"It's not a big deal," she replied, dismissing herself.

But when I asked Cathy how she would feel if, one day, one of her little students was having these sorts of relationships, she was more circumspect. She said, "I wouldn't want that for any of the girls in my class."

"Why is it OK for you?" I asked.

"I mean, I know some of these guys care about me," she said defensively. "Just not enough to be my boyfriend."

"That's sad," I said.

"It's fine." She shrugged as she broke eye contact.

"I don't believe you," I said. "I don't believe it's fine, or that you think it's fine."

The tell was that Cathy was reluctant to talk about men. I'd know nothing about the latest guy until her heart was broken. She would sanitize her description of a first date and only later let it slip that it amounted to little more than a hookup in someone's office. If she were simply enjoying her postmodern sexual freedom, then why all the secrecy?

When I asked Cathy what her best friend of many years had to say about her relationships with men, she seemed confused and stammered, "N-n-nothing... I mean, she doesn't know."

"She doesn't know," I emphasized.

"No," Cathy said, surprising herself with the realization. "It never occurred to me to tell her." This meant something to me. She didn't *choose* not to tell her best friend about her relationships with men; it never even crossed her mind. In my own mind, I flagged shame.

I asked Cathy whom she'd been talking to all these years. "I tell different people tiny bits and pieces. I think the full story would be too much for any one person," she said. "The only completely honest conversations I have are with music."

"How's that?" I pressed.

Cathy said her iPod was loaded with angry, hurt songs. She didn't talk much about how she felt, so she listened to artists who said it all for her. "Sometimes I'm riding the bus to work and I think, 'No one would believe the music I'm listening to right now. No one would believe what's going on in my head,'" she confessed. Like the iPod commercial where the silhouette of a person walks calmly down the street while the shadow dances wildly against a background wall, Cathy cruised through her twenties looking like a happy teacher while her shadow was filled with anger and despair.

When I told Cathy about my association to the iPod commercial, she said that was how life felt for her, split to the point where she could not bring the pieces of herself together. Cathy feared her shadow would take over one day, at exactly the wrong moment, and ruin everything. But she also worried she would forever remain trapped in her pretend appearance of being happy, never truly known by anyone and unable to get out.

One of the most valuable lessons I've learned as a psychotherapist was best stated by a clinician named Masud Khan: The most difficult thing to cure is the patient's attempt at self-cure. Very few lives are perfect and, because young people are generally resilient, many bounce back from difficulties with their own solutions in place. They may be outdated, imperfect solutions, but they are solutions nonetheless—ones that usually resist dismantling.

A self-cure may seem harmless or subtle, such as the way Cathy soothed herself with music and men. Or it may be obviously troubling, like cutting or bingeing or getting high to numb out. Usually sometime during the twentysomething years, life changes and the old solutions seem cumbersome and out of place. The things that once helped us feel better now get in our way. It's not OK to go to work with scars on our arms, and live-in girlfriends get tired of seeing us stoned. But we feel like we can't stop listening to the same music or hooking up for a fleeting moment of attention. A self-cure can take on a life of its own.

"Cathy, there's a proverb that says 'A raft is a good thing to have when you're crossing a river. But when you get to the other side, put it down.'"

"Huh?"

"For a while, music and sex helped you feel less alone, but now they are making you feel more alone. Every problem was once a solution."

"What am I supposed to do?" Cathy asked, almost lost.

"I want you to stop listening to your iPod and start talking to me instead."

"What's wrong with my iPod?"

"Your iPod is whispering in your ear. It was keeping you company, but now it's like a good friend turned bad, keeping you over in the corner away from other relationships where you might learn something new. It is turning your life into a dark, looping rock opera."

"My iPod *is* my friend . . . maybe my closest friend," Cathy said through tears.

"I know. But that's a problem because it can't talk back. It's just confirming every bad thing you already think about yourself and the world. You said the only honest conversations you have are with music. These are conversations you are having with yourself."

"I can't not listen. It's like the soundtrack for my life. It's the story of my life," Cathy said.

"Tell *me* that story."

"Can I give you my soundtrack?"

"I would be honored if you did. But I won't hear the songs the same way you do. Try to tell me the story."

Over some sessions, a story emerged:

> I didn't have a boyfriend in high school. I didn't have sex in high school. People really made fun of me for it. I grew up in this hip Southern town, where the kids were so cool and really wild. I felt so uncool and left out. My parents badgered me to fit in, to be part of the mainstream. I have a lot of energy, you know. I'm spirited, I like to say. My dad was always saying I was too much for everybody. He was always telling me to take it down a notch. My mom was always saying if I dressed better or lost ten pounds guys would like me more. But I was the Asian girl that nobody was going to like no matter what I did.
>
> I went to this small private school and the kids there were super-mean to me. There was no escape. They were cruel and, it probably sounds like an exaggeration, but I felt tortured by them. I begged my parents to let me go to a different school, a bigger one, where at least I could have actually faded into the background. But they would say this was the best school for college prep, blah, blah, and that if I just dressed or acted different, people would like me more.
>
> I don't know why, but being teased about not having sex really bothered me. Maybe because it was such an invasion of my most personal space.

> I felt like Hester Prynne in reverse, walking around with a big V on my chest. I felt so rejected in so many ways.
>
> Three years out of college, I was still a virgin. I felt behind, like it was too late to join in, and that was really hanging me up. So finally, I did it. I was out one night with work friends and I got really drunk and had sex with the lead singer of this band, in the back of a limo actually. That probably seems awful, but it was pretty OK.

Cathy wasn't the only client I've had who held her nose and jumped into the deep end of sex. I kept listening.

"I felt like I joined the world that night," she said. "My whole life, it was like no one noticed me, except for my parents or maybe the kids in high school, and they never liked what they saw. Then all of a sudden I had something people wanted."

"Sex."

"Yeah."

"Is that what you wanted?"

"I wanted to be wanted."

"You wanted to be wanted," I reflected back.

"I'm not proud of it," Cathy admitted. "There's a serious gap in some stuff I do. I'll get into something with somebody and I'll know it's a bad idea. But it's just so easy. It's hard to resist this power handed to me."

"Power..."

"The power to not feel unattractive and insecure. The power to feel special."

"And if a man doesn't want you, you feel unspecial?"

"If someone doesn't want me, I feel awful. My confidence goes down. If there isn't a guy in my life, it's like a desert to me. Each person who wants me feels like an oasis. Like maybe this will be the last person to want me. I feel like I have to drink up. I have to take whatever I can get. If I don't find someone, I view it as being rejected by everyone."

Cathy continued.

"I feel like I have to keep hooking up and see what sticks," she said.

"I'm not sure anything sticks like that," I said.

"Listening to myself say this, I feel like I should have known better than to listen to those people from high school, or to still be listening. But even now if I want to stay home and work on my writing, it can't just be that. It means I'm becoming the crazy cat lady who will never find anyone. I constantly feel like everyone I meet started all this sooner. Like everyone else always wins. At some point, it needs to just be enough. I caught up. I'm not seventeen anymore."

"That's right. You're twenty-seven."

"Twenty-seven. Hearing that, it's hard to believe I'm that old. And saying all this out loud. I have never said all of this to anyone—ever. It's embarrassing to hear me say how much this still controls me. I try not to think about it. I try to keep it in the back of my mind. When is this going to stop running my life?"

"When you get this story out of the back of your mind," I said.

There is a stereotype that psychologists are only interested in childhood memories. Childhood is important, but more and more I am curious about what went on in high school. High school and our twenties are not only the time when we have our most self-defining experiences, study after study shows they are also the time when we have our most self-defining *memories.*

Adolescence is a time of many firsts, including our first attempt to form life stories. As we become capable of—and interested in—abstract thought, we start to put together stories about who we are and why. As our social networks expand across our teens and twenties, we repeat these stories to others and to ourselves. We use them to feel a sense of coherence as we move from place to place.

The stories we tell about ourselves become facets of our identity. They reveal our unique complexity. All at once, they say something about friends, family, and culture. They say something about *why* we live as we do from year to year.

I often help clients build professional identities by crafting stories about themselves that make sense, stories they can take around to job interviews. Personal stories about relationships are much trickier. Without résumés to organize our experiences with friends and lovers, or interviews that require us to reflect, our most intimate self-defining memories can be pieced together in strange, even painful, ways. Though some of these stories may be left untold, they are no less meaningful or powerful. Research—and clinical experience—suggest that these untold stories are most often about shame.

The power of these untold personal stories is that, like for Cathy, they can loop silently in our minds without anyone, sometimes even ourselves, knowing about them. The stories are often found hiding, as Cathy said, in the gaps between what we plan to do and what we actually do, or between what happens and what we tell people about what happens.

Yet these stories are the bits of identity with perhaps the greatest potential for change. Later, we will hear about how personality can change in our twenties—and it can. But it cannot change as quickly, or as dramatically, as the stories we tell about ourselves. Life stories with themes of ruin can trap us. Life stories that are triumphant can transform us. So, part of what I do with clients like Cathy is help them tell their stories. Then we change them.

"Our stories need to be edited and revised over time," I told Cathy. "You of all people ought to understand that."

"Yeah. Seriously."

"Tell me what you know about editing your stories for children."

"Oh. That's the most important part. When you write a story, there are probably some good instincts there, but you're blinded by the feelings of the moment. When you look back on a story later, you can be more objective. A story you wrote might have made sense to you at the time you wrote it, but it has to make sense for everyone who reads it. You can see where it doesn't make sense."

"That's right. The story you are telling yourself now is a first draft left over from adolescence. It doesn't make sense to me."

"It doesn't," Cathy half stated and half asked.

"No, it doesn't. You aren't behind. You aren't unwanted. When are you going to stop dating down?"

"Some of the guys I date are good-looking, I'll have you know..." Cathy responded playfully.

"I'm not talking about looks. I'm sure some of these men are perfectly handsome and nice. But you never challenge them to take you seriously. I'm talking about dating down to an old, low, inaccurate version of yourself."

"I *am*. It's like I'm still that untouchable everybody said I was. Like I'm still seventeen."

"A lot has happened since then."

Twentysomething women and men who are dating down—or working down, for that matter—usually have untold, or at least unedited, stories. These stories originated in old conversations and experiences and, so, they change only through new conversations and new experiences.

As Cathy's therapist, I had a lot of catching up to do. After years of listening to her parents, the kids from high school, and her iPod, Cathy sometimes barely noticed my words—or even her own. Then finally, she came in and said, "I've been working up the courage to ask you something. It's the scariest, most embarrassing question I've ever asked anyone."

I sat waiting for what felt like a long time.

"How do you see me?" Cathy asked, eyes brimming with tears.

This simple question left me with a hollow feeling in my throat. I knew it came from a deep sense of not being seen, from no one ever really looking at Cathy and telling her what they saw. I also knew it meant she was ready to have someone help her rewrite her story.

I told Cathy I saw her as a person who had been made to feel "too much" and "less-than" all at the same time. I told her I was concerned that if she kept dating whoever came along, she might just marry whoever came along at thirty-one or thirty-four. We spent many months talking about who she was now: a twentysomething who'd survived years of teenage rejection and emerged as an enthusiastic and beloved teacher, a budding writer, a beautiful and desirable young woman, a Korean American with special knowledge of what it means not to be seen.

We spent even more months helping her shift from being wanted to *wanting*. Cathy had never thought about what *she* wanted or needed in a partner. She never thought she could do the wanting. She never thought she could take charge of her love life.

"I feel like I've realized this isn't some game," Cathy said. "I'm at the point in my life where my next relationship could be my last one. I mean, let's get real."

"Yes, let's," I said.

Cathy slowed down with men. She took some time in therapy to think about the qualities that were important to her, and to consider what kind of relationship would make her feel good. She started to view dating and sex as enjoyable but serious undertakings where she could learn something about what she wanted in a mate. She started to see that men wanted to be with her, even if she wasn't offering sex up front. "I never thought I could be in relationships like these," she said.

Cathy is still dating, so I don't know what kind of relationship she will ultimately choose. But she makes better decisions on Friday and Saturday nights, ones that are no longer driven by conversations between her and the kids from high school, between her and her parents, or between her iPod and herself. Cathy has new voices in her head—mine, her best friend's, her students', and her own—and these are the people she talks to now. These are the people she listens to now.

Her story is being revised.

Being in Like

People love those who are like themselves.

—Aristotle, philosopher

What counts in making a happy marriage is not so much how compatible you are, but how you deal with incompatibility.

—Leo Tolstoy, writer

Eli was part of the blue-shirt brigade that streams out of the BART stations and into downtown San Francisco every Monday through Friday at about eight forty-five a.m. Each time I saw him, he had on pressed khakis, a dry-cleaned Oxford shirt of some color between pale sky and navy ink, and a holster with various high-tech accoutrements.

Like many men who go to psychotherapy, Eli was sent by his girlfriend, who thought he partied too much. In our first session, Eli dutifully reported his marching orders, but it soon became clear he had other things on his mind. Eli shifted around on the couch and fidgeted with his BlackBerry a lot. He seemed uncomfortable with his own thoughts. He would sit silent for moments at a time. Most clients hate periods of silence because they feel on the spot, but I could often tell that Eli punctuated quiet moments out of concern for me, even though I was the one who was used to them.

Over some months, in a roundabout way, Eli spoke of his own reservations about his girlfriend: She didn't laugh much, she focused endlessly on her dissertation rather than going out and doing things, she seemed somewhat subdued. It bothered Eli that when they went to see his family, it took her a while to feel at ease with everyone and, even when she did, she rarely joined in on the big laughs or the intensely competitive board games. He thought maybe she was depressed. When Eli said something critical about his girlfriend, he quickly undid it, softening any remark by reminding me how sweet she was. He worried about hurting her feelings even though she could not hear us.

Eli and his girlfriend had gotten together quickly, having sex and setting a routine before they really got to know each other. Clearly there was intimacy and loyalty, but I don't think they liked each other very much. From what I could tell, Eli's girlfriend spent her therapy hours being concerned about who Eli was, and I know that Eli spent his therapy hours reluctantly having second thoughts about her. He wanted to be with someone who liked to be playful and someone who enjoyed going out and having fun with family and friends. He imagined someone who woke up happy and headed out to the park for a run.

"What is it you like about your girlfriend?" I asked one day.

"She's really pretty. And we have good sex." This was followed by a long pause.

"Looks and sex. I'm not sure that's enough to sustain a relationship."

"Yeah. I don't know. I guess I want someone... more..."

"Maybe someone more like yourself?"

"Well, that's embarrassing. It makes me sound like I'm in love with myself."

"Eli, compatibility is not some sort of crime."

"It's not?" he chuckled.

"No. It's actually a really good plan."

Eli and his girlfriend were not a particularly good match, but this was not clear to them. They were both good-looking. They were both Jewish and Democrats. They had the same friends and good sex, and the rest they worked around. Both were kindhearted people who wanted to be in a relationship, and they avoided conflict to keep each other happy. Meanwhile, his faithfulness verged on obedience, and her steadiness could be seen as doggedness.

At some point, Eli told me that he and his girlfriend were going to Nicaragua. I was thrilled.

Traveling in a third-world country is the closest thing there is to being married and raising kids. You have glorious hikes and perfect days on the beach. You go on adventures you would never try, or enjoy, alone. But you also can't get away from each other. Everything is unfamiliar. Money is tight or you get robbed. Someone gets sick or sunburned. You get bored. It is harder than you expected, but you are glad you didn't just sit home. Provided Eli did not pop the question by some picturesque waterfall, this was exactly what he and his girlfriend needed. They needed to see how they traveled together.

When Eli returned, he was crestfallen. Under the chronic stress of Nicaragua, he and his girlfriend had become more extreme versions of who they already were. She wanted to go on daylong walks to the ruins, while Eli wanted to hang out in the towns and restaurants. She wanted to stick to a travel budget, while Eli wanted to feel carefree. Eli had been looking forward to a side trip into Costa Rica when he became ill and needed help, which apparently she did not do a good job of providing. Their time and money pooled, it wasn't so easy to part ways out of convenience. They spent many nights sleeping in separate beds, listening to the birds and monkeys in the rain forest. The relationship ended soon after the trip.

Eli and his girlfriend needed to be "in like." By this I mean two things: being *alike* in ways that matter and genuinely *liking* who the other person is. Often these go hand in hand. That is because the more similar two people are, the more they are able to understand each other. Each appreciates how the other acts and how he or she goes about the day, and this forestalls an incredible amount of friction. Two people who are similar are going to have the same reactions to a rainy day, a new car, a long vacation, an anniversary, a Sunday morning, and a big party.

We sometimes hear that opposites attract, and maybe they do for a hookup. More often, similarity is the essence of compatibility. Studies have repeatedly found that couples who are similar in areas such as socioeconomic status, education, age, ethnicity, religion, attractiveness, attitudes, values, and intelligence are more likely to be satisfied with their relationships and are less likely to seek divorce.

Finding someone like you might seem easy, but there is a twist—not just any similarity will do. Dating and married couples *do* tend to be similar to each other in attractiveness, age, education, political views, religion, and intelligence. So what about all those divorces out there? What about Eli and his girlfriend? The problem is, while people are good at matching themselves and others on relatively obvious criteria, such as age and education, it turns out that these qualities are what researchers call "deal breakers, not match makers."

Deal breakers are your own personal *sine qua non* in relationships. They are qualities—almost always similarities—you feel are nonnegotiable. The absence of these similarities allows you to weed out people with whom you have fundamental differences. Maybe it is a deal breaker if someone is not Christian because you want to share spirituality and community. Perhaps you cannot imagine being with someone who is not intellectually curious because you value enriching conversation in your relationships. Sometimes people can even agree to disagree about very apparent, circumscribed differences, like Republican-Democrat couples who joke about their "mixed marriages." Either way, people decide for themselves early on what their own deal breakers are, and, typically, we select partners accordingly. But these conspicuous similarities are not match makers. They may bring us together, but they don't necessarily make us happy.

One match maker to consider is personality. Some research tells us that, especially in young couples, the more similar two people's personalities are, the more likely they are to be satisfied with their relationship. Yet personality is how dating, and even married, couples tend to be least alike. The likely reason for this is, unlike deal breakers, personality is less obvious and not as easy to categorize. Personality is not about *what* we have done or even about *what* we like. It is about *how* we are in the world, and this infuses everything we do. Personality is the part of ourselves that we take everywhere, even to Nicaragua, so it is worth knowing something about.

The Big Five

Several years ago, I started to notice some particularly well-matched couples in my practice and in my social circle—people who, no matter how quirky or complex, had found someone who seemed similarly quirky and complex. When these couples would tell their stories about finding each other, the punch line was always "We met online!" and everyone around would say, "Isn't that amazing?" The more I learned about what exactly they meant, the less amazing it seemed. These couples weren't talking about meeting in chat rooms or posting personal ads, they were talking about being *matched* online.

While some Internet dating sites are nothing more than electronic bulletin boards for personals and photos, others purportedly assess your personality and pair you with similar others. These sorts of sites say they are more concerned with who you are than with what you want. This is good. The "what you want" questions bring us back to the deal breakers—hobbies, religion, politics, and other similarities that, while convenient, may not actually make us happy. The "who you are" questions are about profiling your personality. Some research suggests that couples who were matched through this sort of service tend to be happier than couples who meet in other ways, and if these matching sites are pairing people based on their personality profiles, then this makes some sense.

I understand that the success of online dating sites is as variable as their methods. Besides, not everyone is interested in meeting on the Internet. Nevertheless, I do like that this sort of approach brings personality to the forefront sooner rather than later—during dating rather than during divorce counseling. That's something everyone ought to do, and something that everyone can do.

You don't need a fancy test to think about your personality or anyone else's. One of the simplest and most widely researched models of personality is what is called the Big Five. The Big Five refers to five factors that describe how people interact with the world: Openness, Conscientiousness, Extraversion, Agreeableness, Neuroticism. Just by reading about the Big Five and considering your own behavior, it is pretty easy to tell whether you fall on the high end or the low end, or somewhere in the middle, of the five dimensions.

The Big Five is not about what you like—it is about who you are, it is about *how* you live. The Big Five tells us how you wake up in the morning and how you go about doing most anything. It has to do with how you experience the world and, as a result, how others experience you. This is important because, when it comes to personality, wherever you go, there you are.

Consider that where we are on the Big Five is about 50 percent inherited. This means that you came into this world with roughly half of who you are already in place, because

The Big Five

	LOW	HIGH
OPENNESS	practical, conventional, prefers routine, skeptical, rational, shies away from new things	open to new experiences, intellectually curious, creative, imaginative, adventurous, insightful
CONSCIENTIOUSNESS	relaxed about standards, easygoing, can be careless, spontaneous, prone to addiction	disciplined, efficient, organized, responsible, dutiful, self-directed, thorough, can be controlling
EXTRAVERSION	likes solitary time, shy, reserved, energized by being alone, quiet, independent, cautious, aloof	outgoing, enthusiastic, active, novelty-seeking, gets energy from interactions with others, talkative
AGREEABLENESS	uncooperative, antagonistic, suspicious, has trouble understanding others	cooperative, kind, affectionate, friendly, compassionate, trusting, compliant, understanding
NEUROTICISM	not easily bothered, secure, takes things at face value, emotionally resilient	tense, moody, anxious, sensitive, prone to sadness, worries a lot, quickly sees the negative

of genes, prenatal influences, and other biological factors. While you learn to interact with the world somewhat differently as experiences make their mark, personality remains relatively stable over time. Any parent can attest to the power of personality: "David has been that way since the day he was born" or, about siblings, "Avery and Hannah have been completely different since day one."

When you figure out your highs, mediums, and lows, you have a general profile of your personality, one that should describe your behavior across different situations and times. You can do the same for anyone that you know well, or are starting to know well, and this will bring into relief how similar—or dissimilar—your personalities are. There is no right or wrong personality, there is just *your* personality and how it fits with the personalities of other people. While it is not better or worse to be high or low or in the middle of the dimensions of the Big Five, it is often the case that we like or dislike people because of the way their extremes compare to our own.

From what I could tell, Eli didn't party too much. It also didn't sound like Eli's girlfriend was clinically depressed. Sometimes the only thing wrong with another person is that he or she is a poor match for your own personality.

From what we know in this chapter, we can see that Eli is very active and approaching. He likes getting up early and heading out into the world. He's often in a good mood and loves loud stories but does not care for time constraints or routines. This tells me Eli is relatively high on Openness and Extraversion but somewhat low on Conscientiousness and Neuroticism.

We can only see Eli's girlfriend through his eyes, but he

described her as someone who, largely in contrast to himself, is withdrawing and responsible. It takes her a while to warm up to new situations, but once she is involved in something she can be very focused and goal-oriented. She sounds like the opposite of Eli, low on Openness and Extraversion but high on Conscientiousness and Neuroticism. Fortunately, Eli and his girlfriend both sounded high on Agreeableness, which probably had a lot to do with why they stayed together as long as they did.

Eli and his girlfriend did not understand each other. They were fooled into thinking they were compatible because they had many plain-sight commonalities. They felt confused as their dissimilar personalities continually clashed. Not sure what to make of this, each hoped the other might change. Both imagined that they might become more similar the longer they were together, but the evidence for personality convergence over time is mixed.

Sometimes dating or married couples decide to split because things change—someone cheated or had to move—but, more often, people split up because things don't change. It is far more common to hear couples say that, in retrospect, the differences were there all along.

When and if you commit, chances are that you will choose someone who is similar to you in ways that are convenient. But long-term relationships are inevitably inconvenient. Psychologist Daniel Gilbert calls them "the gateway to hard work" as they open the door to mortgages, children, and the like. Personality tells us something about *how* you and your partner will go about the good and bad days together.

Your Big Five won't match exactly, of course, but the more similar your personalities, the smoother things may be. And for all of the ways you may not be like someone you love, by knowing something about his or her personality you have the opportunity to be more understanding about why he or she does the very different (or annoying) things that he or she does. That goes a long way toward bridging differences, and that's important too.

* * *

"My boyfriend has an engagement ring in a drawer at his apartment," Courtney said, the first time she sat down on my couch. "I'm twenty-eight and I want to get married. I think. But I feel like I've been diving behind furniture, avoiding moments he could propose, because I don't know if I want to say yes."

"Oh?" I said, sitting up straight in my chair, thinking how glad I was to be having this conversation *before* the wedding. "Do you know why not?"

For approximately five minutes, Courtney dispensed with what was right about Matt: He was devoted to her, had a good job as a microbiologist, was handsome, had a good heart, was sexually in tune with her, worked hard to please her, and he loved her. Courtney enjoyed being with Matt, he made her happy, and she loved him.

Then, over the next several sessions, I heard what was wrong about Matt: Maybe he wasn't tall enough. Sometimes he wasn't funny enough at parties. He didn't like to talk about life as much as she did. He didn't bring her lilies on her birthday even though her best friend told him to. He wasn't the best dresser. His mother kept sending corny scrapbooks she made from Matt and Courtney's online photos.

Courtney gestured imploringly during most of her stories, but I noticed I did not find her complaints to be compelling. After a few weeks I said, "I'm confused, Courtney.

I've been listening to you carefully for some time now and you seem clearly anxious and worked up. But I keep asking myself, 'Are these foundational incompatibilities we're talking about, or are you not letting you and Matt be different?'"

Courtney's head snapped back. I could see my question surprised her.

"But the cheesy scrapbooks, *puh-lease*!" Courtney furthered, searching my face for the laughs it seemed she was used to getting.

"What young couple doesn't have a closet full of crap from relatives?" I asked sincerely.

Courtney's anxiety about Matt—and about me—grew. The same book had been sitting unread on Matt's nightstand for months; what did that mean? He didn't like to do things outdoors; what if he wasn't rugged enough? Meanwhile, she noticed she didn't like the way I started sessions by sitting silent, and my wedding ring made her wonder if I was too conservative to understand her point of view.

Maybe she needed a new boyfriend *and* a new therapist, Courtney thought aloud. Maybe so, I acknowledged. But I had noticed Matt didn't sound as lame as she made him out to be. As a matter of fact, when she wasn't busy scanning for what might be wrong with him, the days and nights they spent together actually sounded quite nice.

As I listened to Courtney, I spent some of the time thinking about the Big Five and relationships. Yet rather than wondering whether she and Matt were similar enough to be reasonably compatible (which it actually sounded like they were), I kept thinking of an even more robust research finding: that being on the high end of the Neuroticism dimension is toxic for relationships.

Neuroticism, or the tendency to be anxious, stressed, critical, and moody, is far more predictive of relationship unhappiness and dissolution than is personality dissimilarity. While personality similarity can help the years run smoothly, any two people will be different in some way or another. How a person responds to these differences can be more important than the differences themselves. To a person who runs high in Neuroticism, differences are seen in a negative light. Anxiety and judgments about these differences then lead to criticism and contempt, two leading relationship killers.

Courtney sometimes came to appointments armed with e-mails from her best friend, such as one that said she ought to "run, not walk" and another that said she ought to refuse to settle for Matt.

"You don't have to marry Matt, but if you did, how would that be settling?" I asked.

"Because he doesn't remember to bring me lilies. He doesn't read the newspaper! I mean, what does that say about his intellect?"

"I thought he was quite successful as a microbiologist. Doesn't that say something about his intellect?"

Courtney ignored me and went on. "Still. My best friend says the whole lilies thing is a bad sign."

"Is this friend married?" I asked.

"No," Courtney replied.

I flashed to a story of my own.

My first child was born via cesarean section after I went into labor almost three days earlier. When it was all over, the doctors told me to cozy up to my new baby and to the button that dispensed pain medication; I would be able to eat in a day or so. Then they told my husband to go get some food for himself. A short time later, he came back to my hospital room with one piece of pizza, one beer, one chocolate-chip cookie, and one ice-cream sandwich. When I spotted his food, I was ready to scream.

My aunt, who had come to the hospital to help with the baby, quickly whisked my husband out of the room and into the cafeteria. When she returned, it was simple for me to make a case against him. *I* would never visit some sick person in the hospital and chow down on my lunch while he or she sat there unable to eat. Surely this meant *my* life was changing because of the baby while his was staying the same.

My aunt listened for a while. Then she said gently, "Meg, honey, I think your standards are too high."

"Yours are too low!" I shot back, thinking of the nights my aunt cooked for my uncle before she went out to dinner with her friends, or of the times my uncle sat reading his book while she ran herself ragged. She was selling me out, I thought.

Years later, I can see we were both right. My aunt is from a different generation and she has accepted a division of labor that would not suit me. But I *was* being unfair to my husband. He'd been awake for seventy-two hours also. He'd stood by my side through labor and major surgery. He'd worried about the well-being of his wife and baby for days. The doctor did tell him to go eat, and he'd quickly brought his food back to the room so he could be with me. (And the flowers were delivered just moments after he was ushered to the cafeteria.)

Now, I chalk up my own bad behavior toward my husband (and toward my aunt) to pain and exhaustion, and to not recognizing that my husband and I were responding in different ways to being stressed. He made himself feel better by eating something yummy because he could. I got angry because I couldn't. That's all.

I said to Courtney, "I'm thinking about all you have to say, both as a psychologist who knows the research and as a married person who knows what marriage is like. I'm not sure how germane lilies and soul-baring talks will be to your relationship ten years from now. Soon life will be happening and you'll probably be too busy, and maybe even too happy, to spend your time deconstructing it."

"Hopefully," she chuckled.

"I think it's easy to surround yourself with friends who are just like you. As a group, you may decide everyone else is doing it wrong. Friends can form a culture of criticism where differences are seen as deficiencies."

"OK..."

"But sometimes differences are just differences. They can even be strengths."

Research on long-term marriages suggests what we need in marriage changes over time. It is a young couple's job to create a shared vision and a shared life. When this is the task, similarities can feel validating and comforting, and differences can feel threatening. By our forties and beyond, as work, children, home, activities, extended family, and community come to the fore, marriage is typically less couple-centered. When couples are juggling more than dinners and shared weekends, a diversification of skills and interests can be helpful. Differences can keep life fresh.

"So you're telling me not to be picky."

"I'm challenging you to be picky about things that might matter in twenty years, such as extreme differences in values or goals or personality—or whether you love each other. But the differences you're sounding off about seem like everyday discrepancies that are part of any real relationship."

"But that's the thing. How do I know if a relationship is hard because it's wrong or because it's real?"

"You'll never know with complete certainty. That's why marriage is a commitment, not a guarantee."

"Then how can I ever choose someone?"

"The same way you make any decision. You weigh the evidence and you listen to yourself. The trick for you is going to be to listen to what matters, not to every single thing that makes you dissatisfied or anxious."

"OK."

"There will always be differences of some kind but, statistically speaking, that's not what will kill a relationship. It's what you do with the differences. Do you know what the differences are going in? Have you thought about how they will affect your life? Are you prepared to bridge or even accept them?"

"Those questions make me really nervous."

"Then let's ask some different questions. Let's say you and Matt break up. What happens if that perfect match does not exist?"

"Fair question."

"To continue being fair, let's try this the other way too. Let's say you keep looking and you find that perfect mate. What happens when you have a daughter or a son who isn't so perfect, who doesn't do things like you do? Back to criticism and contempt?"

Courtney added a joke. "That—or the other day I actually had a brief thought about adopting an older child so I can find the perfect match in a kid."

I didn't laugh. I've worked with too many kids raised on criticism and contempt.

Courtney suffered a severe knee injury from running. Two months later, she hobbled back into my office on crutches, looking humbled. "I think I might want to marry Matt," she said.

"Oh really?" I said, surprised.

"Yeah. I've had a lot of time to think. Matt has been amazing. He took off work and carted me to every doctor appointment and surgery you can imagine. And we had some really good talks during all this."

"How wonderful."

"The biggest talk came after my best friend sent me this big bunch of lilies. I was upset Matt didn't do something like that. He got angry and pointed out how she hadn't even been over to my apartment to help but he'd done everything he could to take care of me. I realized Matt was right. He'd done everything for me, no complaints. I realized I'm the complainer and he doesn't even complain about that."

"Wow."

"I told him I saw the engagement ring in his drawer and I thought I probably did want to get married but I wanted some more time. He said he wants to surprise me and ask when I'm not expecting it, but we agreed we would wait one year."

"And what's the year for?"

"I want to use this time to really look at my relationship with Matt and to look at myself."

"I see," I said.

"I came here because I thought Matt had to do all the changing if we were going to get married. Now I see that, whether I decide to be with Matt or not, there are things I need to change about myself. I need to get my emotions under control. But what if I can't change? What if it's too late for me?"

Courtney was realizing her personality was her real challenge, that that's what her work in therapy was going to be about. "It's not too late," I said. "But, whatever it is you want to change about yourself, now is the time to change it."

THE BRAIN AND THE BODY

Forward Thinking

Life can only be understood backward, but it must be lived forward.

—Søren Kierkegaard, philosopher

The more you use your brain, the more brain you will have to use.

—George A. Dorsey, anthropologist

In 1848, Phineas Gage was a twenty-five-year-old railway worker, building the bed for the Rutland & Burlington Railroad in Vermont. On Wednesday, September 13, of that year, he and his crew were blasting through a rocky outcrop in order to create a flat surface for the rails. Gage's job was to drill holes in the rock, fill the holes with gunpowder, add sand, and then pack the sand and gunpowder down with a tamping iron. Later, fuses would be lit to explode the rock. The tamping iron was three feet long and about a quarter inch wide at the narrow end, and about one inch wide at the fat end.

At four thirty p.m. on that day, Phineas Gage drilled a hole and added gunpowder. In this particular hole, he forgot to add sand. As he packed the gunpowder down with his tamping iron, sparks from the rod striking the rock ignited the gunpowder, causing an explosion that drove the tamping iron out of Gage's hand and through his head. The rod entered Gage's head point-first under the left cheekbone. It passed behind the left eye socket and exited through the top of his skull.

After the accident, Phineas Gage was—and was not—fine. To the amazement of his coworkers, Gage was alive and could talk. He rode upright in an oxcart to the nearest town and greeted the summoned physician with "Doctor, here is business enough for you." Although in the mid-1800s scientists were not sure how the brain worked, it was generally thought to be central to life and movement. But here was Phineas Gage, walking and talking with a hole through his head. After some time, Gage was examined by doctors at Harvard. He then traveled to New York City and around New England, where he told his story and displayed himself to curious onlookers.

Over time it became clear that not all was well with Phineas Gage. Those around him were so impressed he was alive, it took a while to notice he was no longer acting like himself. Before the accident, he had been a "great favorite" among friends, an "efficient and capable" worker, and in possession of "temperate habits" and "a well-balanced mind." After the accident, he was suddenly wavering about plans for the future. Phineas Gage now said and did what he wanted with little concern for others or the consequences. His doctor concluded that "the balance between his intellectual faculties and animal propensities seems to have been destroyed." His friends and family said he was so altered, he was "no longer Gage."

Gage's condition suggested that, while the forward part of the brain may not have much to do with whether we live and breathe, it has a lot to do with how we act. It would be more than a hundred years before scientists would understand how.

After Gage's accident, scientists raced to map the brain. It was difficult to do research on humans, so, as in the case of Phineas Gage, doctors had to rely on whatever injuries and illnesses came their way. This all changed in the 1970s when magnetic resonance imaging (MRI) and then functional MRI (fMRI) technology made it possible for doctors to look at the brain *in vivo*. A host of new technologies can now measure brain activity in living children and adults, and this has allowed researchers to better understand how the brain works.

We now know that the brain develops from bottom to top and from back to front. This order reflects the evolutionary age of the areas of the brain. The oldest parts of the brain—the ones also present in our ancient ancestors and animal cousins—develop first, at the base of the brain near the spine. They control breathing, senses, emotions, sex, pleasure, sleep, hunger and thirst, or the "animal propensities" left intact after Phineas Gage's injury. Roughly speaking, these areas are what we consider to be the emotional brain.

The most forward part of the brain—literally and figuratively—is the frontal lobe, located just behind the forehead. The most recent part of the brain to have evolved in humans, it is also the final area of the brain to mature in each individual. Nicknamed the "executive functioning center" and the "seat of civilization," the frontal lobe is where reason and judgment reside. It is where rational thoughts balance, and regulate, the feelings and impulses of the emotional brain.

The area of the brain that processes probability and time, the frontal lobe is also where we tackle uncertainty. This allows us to think not only about the present but also about the future. It is where we quiet our emotions long enough to anticipate the likely consequences of our behavior and plan accordingly for tomorrow, even though no outcome is certain and the future is unknown. This front part of the brain is where we do our forward thinking.

Consider twentieth- and twenty-first-century patients with frontal lobe damage, several of whom have been written about extensively. What stands out about these patients is that, although their intellect is unchanged and their ability to solve concrete problems remains intact, they show significant deficits in personal and social decision-making. They make choices in friends, partners, and activities that go against their own best interests. They find it difficult to see an abstract goal in terms of the concrete steps needed to reach it. They have trouble planning their days and their years.

If this sounds familiar, it should. Modern advances and modern patients have largely solved the mystery of Phineas Gage. In the mid-1800s, it was inconceivable that someone could suffer a brain injury and live to tell about it, and that this same person could do some things but not others. We now understand that Phineas Gage changed from thoughtful to reckless, from purposeful to vacillating, because the tamping rod had made a hole in his frontal lobe.

Twentysomethings might have little reason to care about Phineas Gage and the frontal lobe if not for researchers at the Laboratory of Neuro Imaging at UCLA. From MRI scans of healthy adolescents and twentysomethings, we now know that the frontal lobe does not fully mature until sometime between the ages of twenty and thirty. In our twenties, the pleasure-seeking, emotional brain is ready to go while the forward-thinking frontal lobe is still a work in progress.

Twentysomethings aren't brain damaged, of course, but because of the still-developing frontal lobe, they can be what psychologists call "uneven." Many of my clients are confused by the fact that they went to good colleges, yet they don't know how to start the careers they want. Or they don't understand how they could have been valedictorians but are unable to make decisions about whom to date and why. Or they feel like fakes because they managed to get good jobs yet cannot calm themselves down at work. Or they can't figure out how twentysomethings who did not do as well in school are now outpacing them in life.

These are different skill sets.

Being smart in school is about how well you solve problems that have correct answers and clear time limits. But being a forward-thinking adult is about how you think and act even (and especially) in uncertain situations. The frontal lobe doesn't just allow us to coolly solve the problem of what exactly we should do with our lives. Adult dilemmas—which job to take, where to live, whom to partner with, or when to start a family—don't have right answers. The frontal lobe is where we move beyond the futile search for black-and-white solutions as we learn to tolerate—and act on—better shades of gray.

The late-maturing frontal lobe might seem like a good reason to postpone action, to wait until thirty after all to get started on a life. A recent newspaper article even suggested that maybe twentysomething brains ought to afford them special services of some kind. But dumbing down the twenties is hardly the way to go.

Forward thinking doesn't just come with age. It comes with practice and experience. That's why some twenty-two-year-olds are incredibly self-possessed, future-oriented people who already know how to face the unknown, while some thirty-four-year-olds still have brains that run the other way. To make sense of how people can develop so differently, it helps to know the rest of the story of Phineas Gage.

Phineas Gage's post-injury life has largely been sensationalized. In textbooks, he is most often painted as a loser or freak who ran off and joined the circus, never regaining any semblance of normal life. Gage did briefly exhibit the tamping rod—and himself—at Barnum's American Museum. But more significant, and less widely known, is that before dying after a series of seizures nearly twelve years after the accident, Gage worked for many years as a stagecoach driver, in New Hampshire and Chile. In this work, he rose early and readied himself. He prepared his horses and his coach for four-a.m. daily departures. He drove passengers over rough roads for hours at a time. This is all at odds with the notion that Gage lived out his life as an impulsive slacker.

Historian Malcolm Macmillan suggests that Phineas Gage benefited from a sort of "social recovery." The regular routines of stagecoach driving allowed Gage's frontal lobe to relearn many of the skills compromised in the accident. The experiences he had, day in and day out, allowed Gage to again be personally and socially deliberate, to again be forward-thinking.

Thus, Phineas Gage provided doctors not only with some of the earliest information about the functional areas of the brain but also with some of the earliest evidence of the brain's plasticity. Gage's social recovery, and countless subsequent studies of the brain, tell us that the brain changes in response to the environment. This is especially true in the twentysomething years as the brain caps off its second—and final—growth spurt.

By the time we reach our twenties, the brain has gotten as big as it is going to be, but it is still refining its network of connections. Communication in the brain takes place at the level of the neuron, and the brain is made up of about one hundred billion of these, each of which can make thousands of different connections. Speed and efficiency are paramount and are the hard-won result of two critical periods of growth.

In the first eighteen months of life, the brain experiences its first growth spurt, producing far more neurons than it can use. The infant brain overprepares, readying itself for whatever life brings, such as to speak any language within earshot. This is how we go from being one-year-olds who understand fewer than one hundred words to being six-year-olds who know more than ten thousand.

But this same rapid overproduction of neurons creates an overly crowded network, and this leads to cognitive inefficiency, which is not adaptive. That's why these same spongelike toddlers struggle to string together a few words in a sentence, and they forget to put on their socks before their shoes. Potential and confusion rule the day. To make neural networks more efficient, this first growth spurt is followed by pruning. Across years, the brain keeps the neurons and connections that are used while those that are neglected are pruned, or allowed to die off.

It was long thought that pruning continued in a linear fashion throughout life as the brain refined its neural network. But in the 1990s, researchers at the National Institute of Mental Health discovered that the process repeats itself in a second critical period, one that starts in adolescence and ends in the twentysomething years. Again, thousands of new connections sprout, exponentially increasing our capacity for new learning. Only now the learning isn't about vocabulary or socks and shoes.

Most of the thousands of new connections that sprout in adolescence do so in the frontal lobe and, again, the brain overprepares—but, this time, for the uncertainty of adult life. Early childhood may be the time for language, but evolutionary theorists say this critical period primes us to learn about the complex challenges of adulthood: how to find a professional niche, how to choose and live with a mate, how to be a parent, where and when to stake our claims. This last critical period is rapidly wiring us for adulthood.

But how?

In the same way that young children learn to speak English or French or Catalan or Chinese—whatever the environment offers up—in our twenties we are especially sensitive to whatever is within earshot. Twentysomething jobs teach us about regulating our emotions and negotiating the complicated social interactions that make up adult life. Twentysomething work and school are our best chance to acquire the technical, sophisticated skills needed in so many careers today. Twentysomething relationships are prepping us for marriage and other partnerships. Twentysomething plans help us think across the years and decades ahead. How we learn to cope with twentysomething setbacks readies us for handling our spouses and bosses and children. We even know that larger social networks change our brains for the better as they require us to communicate with more and different others.

As "neurons that fire together, wire together," the jobs we have and the company we keep are rewiring our frontal lobes—and these same frontal lobes are, in turn, making our decisions in the office and on Saturday nights. Back and forth it goes, as work and love and the brain knit together in the twenties to make us into the adults we want to be in our thirties and beyond.

Or not.

Because our twenties are the capstone of this last critical period, they are, as one neurologist said, a time of "great risk and great opportunity." The post-twentysomething brain is still plastic, of course, but the opportunity is that never again in our lifetime will the brain offer up countless new connections and see what we make of them. Never again will we be so quick to learn new things. Never again will it be so easy to become the people we hope to be. The risk is that we may not act now.

In a use-it-or-lose-it fashion, the new frontal lobe connections we use are preserved and quickened; those we don't use just waste away through pruning. We become what we hear and see and do every day. We don't become what we don't hear and see and do every day. In neuroscience, this is known as "survival of the busiest."

Twentysomethings who use their brains by engaging with good jobs and real relationships are learning the language of adulthood just when their brains are primed to learn it. In the chapters ahead, we will see how they learn to calm themselves down at work and in love, and this brings mastery and success. They learn to get along and get ahead, and this makes them happier and more confident. They learn to be forward thinking before life's defining moments are in the rearview mirror. Twentysomethings who don't use their brains become thirtysomethings who feel behind as professionals and as partners—and as people, and they miss out on making the most of life still to come.

It is easy to feel overwhelmed by uncertainty, to want to lie low with the urban tribe, or our parents, until our brains just mature on their own and somehow suddenly know the sure answers to our lives. But that's not how the brain works. And that's not how life works. Besides, even if our brains could wait, love and work can't. The twenties are, indeed, the time to get busy. It's forward thinking for an uncertain age.

Calm Yourself

When we try to do something new, we don't know what we're doing. That's the biggest challenge.

—Jeffrey Kalmikoff, designer

Blown about by every wind of criticism.

—Samuel Johnson, writer

On paper, what I do looks really, really good, but I really, really hate my job." That's what I heard through the phone. And tears. "Just tell me I can quit. If I know I can quit, then I can make it one more day. Just tell me I can quit. That I won't be doing this forever."

"You definitely won't be doing this forever, and of course you can quit. But I don't think you should."

Sniff.

Danielle was a former client who, after working her way through a web of internships and contacts, had become the assistant to one of the biggest names in television news. For a brief moment she thought she had it made. Within a few weeks, she felt worse than ever. We resumed our weekly sessions, this time over the phone. She called every Monday morning at eight a.m. from New York City as she braved heading into the office.

Danielle's job was a cross between *The Devil Wears Prada* and *Entourage.* Her boss yelled at her almost every day, usually because Danielle failed to be omniscient. How *dare* Danielle not know that Mr. X is always put right through on the phone? And *why* did Danielle not foresee that her boss might be bumped from first class?

Worst was when her boss ventured beyond New York City in his own car and got lost among the townships of Connecticut or New Jersey. He would call Danielle at the office and scream into the phone, "*Where the hell am I?!*" as if Danielle could possibly know, sitting at her desk on the verge of what felt like a panic attack.

Danielle's situation may seem extreme or somehow unlikely. Her boss sounded more like a movie character than a real person. But he was a real person, and so was Danielle. We all have these stories.

When I was a graduate student, one of my supervisors was a renowned clinician. It was an honor to be assigned to her, yet I'd heard she was a busy lady who had a problem with multitasking. According to departmental lore, she favored doing supervision in her car as she drove all over town, picking up her dry cleaning and stopping by the bank. This year would be different, the clinic director told me. The supervisor was under strict orders not to leave her office during the supervision hour. How bad could it be?

Our weekly meeting was just after lunch on Tuesdays. The supervisor usually hurried late into her office, carrying a satchel stuffed full of the things she was going to do besides listen to me. Sometimes it was knitting. Other times she sent faxes or dusted her office. Once she had someone come in to reupholster her couch.

One afternoon after we sat down, I watched her reach into her satchel, wondering what it would be this time. First she pulled out a bag of onions. Then a cutting board. Then a butcher's knife. For our entire hour, she chopped onions on the cutting board on her lap as I told her about my clients and she gave me her input. She never once looked my way except at the end of the session to say "Time's up!" Only then did she notice the tears streaming down my face, mostly because of the onions but probably partly because of how I felt.

"Oh! Was this bothering you?" she asked.

All I could do was smile and say, "What are you making?"

Apparently, my supervisor was having a dinner party. She had sessions that stretched into the early evening, so was doing the food prep at her office. As I said good-bye, I acted as if this were the most normal thing in the world. Maybe it was. We all have difficult, even outlandish, work experiences we have to find a way through.

When twentysomethings enter the workforce, and I mean *really* enter the workforce by getting a job that isn't safe or easy, they are in for a shock. With no freshman class to huddle in, they may find themselves all alone at the absolute bottom. At the top may be bosses, like Danielle's, who are in positions of power because of their talent or experience rather than their managerial skills or even their GPAs. Some bosses are not interested in being mentors. Others don't know how. These very same bosses are often the ones who are tasked with teaching twentysomethings how to navigate the brand-new world of work. It may be a match made in hell, but that's the way it is.

As one human resources professional said to me, "I wish someone would tell twentysomethings that the office has a completely different culture than what they are used to. You can't start an e-mail with 'Hey!' You're probably going to have to work at one thing for quite a while before being promoted—or even complimented. People are going to tell you not to tweet about work or put stupid posts on your Gchat status. Not to wear certain clothes. You have to think about how you speak and write. How you act. Twentysomethings who've never had jobs don't know this. Neither do the scanners and baristas who've been hanging out at work chatting with their friends."

What happens at work every day *matters.* Typos matter and sick days matter, not just for the worker but for the company's bottom line. As Danielle said, "I didn't worry like this in school because in a way I knew it didn't mean anything. I wasn't going to fail out, and as long as I made decent grades I was going to walk away with a diploma just like everyone else. The end point was the same. Now what I do makes a difference for my boss and everyone else here. That's what I lose sleep over. Every day I feel like I'm going to be fired. Or I'm going to disappoint someone. They are going to figure out they don't need me. That I don't belong here. Like I've lied on my résumé or something and I'm just pretending to be a grown-up. Then I'll be waiting tables somewhere."

Danielle wasn't fired. She was given more responsibility. In college, Danielle had interned at a television station, so when she wasn't chasing down lattes for her boss, she was allowed to produce the small bits of news no one watched: the feature about the cat stuck in a tree in Central Park or the seasonal story about the Fourth of July fireworks.

Her friends and family said she was doing well to have such a good job. But Danielle didn't feel so well. She loved the work (the producing, not the lattes), but she had never felt so anxious and incompetent in her life. She called herself "the accidental producer." Her confidence was "at an all-time low."

Danielle was right where she needed to be. Twentysomethings who *don't* feel anxious and incompetent at work are usually overconfident or underemployed. Danielle was interested in producing, and this job was her chance. The problem was that, like most twentysomethings, Danielle made mistakes. She sent an e-mail with the wrong tone to a superior. She laid the camera bag over part of a microphone so one of her segments sounded muffled. Sometimes her voice cracked when she spoke in meetings.

When these things happened, some senior employee would breeze by in the hallway and, almost as an afterthought, let Danielle know about her "major screwup." She would sometimes be called into her boss's office, such as when she misspelled a former president's name on a web headline: "We *cannot* afford to piss off half the country—much less the red half," her boss said gravely.

Danielle was describing the everyday microtraumas that can feel a part of the twentysomething workweek. She often felt jolted by bad things that happened, and this took a toll.

She stopped eating breakfast because she felt too queasy before work. At night, she had trouble falling asleep, as she turned over in her mind comments from her boss or anticipated reprimands to come. "Walking around at work is like living in London during the Blitz," she said. "I'm always thinking, 'So far so good,' or how many more hours I need to get through before I'm safe for the day."

Danielle sounded a lot like the other twentysomethings I know who have good jobs. To understand what it can be like to be a twentysomething at work, it helps to know more about how the brain—and the twentysomething brain in particular—processes information.

Evolutionary theorists believe the brain is designed to pay special attention to what catches us off-guard, so we can be better prepared to meet the world next time. The brain even has a built-in novelty detector, a part that sends chemical signals to stimulate memory when new and different things happen. We know from research studies that when people view slides of ordinary objects (such as a house) and bizarre objects (such as a zebra head attached to a car), the viewers are more likely to remember the bizarre. Likewise, when research subjects are startled, such as by the image and sound of a snake, they have better recall for the slides that immediately follow the snake than they do for other slides. Similarly, people are more likely to remember highly emotional events, such as times when they were happy or sad or embarrassed.

When something surprising happens, especially if it arouses emotions, we tend to remember it—vividly—for a long time. These remembrances are called flashbulb memories because they feel illuminated and frozen in time, like our brain has taken a photograph of the moment. That is why most of us remember exactly where we were on the morning of 9/11, just as our parents and grandparents remember what they were doing when they heard President Kennedy had been shot.

Because our twenties are when we transition into so many new things, twentysomething life is full of new and surprising moments, even flashbulb memories. In fact, multiple studies have shown that more vivid memories come from early adulthood than any other developmental stage. Some of these memories are unusually happy, such as getting a dream job or going on a great first date. Other surprising moments are especially difficult, such as hitting Reply All on an e-mail intended for one person, or waiting a miserably long week for the results of an STD test after a night of unprotected sex, or being dumped via text message.

In one of the first college classes I taught, I think I was twenty-eight, I handed back exams—to three hundred people—without recording the grades. That's a mistake you make only once. Everyone learns things the hard way at some time or another, and our brains take pictures so the learning stays with us. This is the basis for the saying "That's a lesson you'll never forget." It is a jarring—but efficient and often necessary—way to grow.

Twentysomethings take these difficult moments particularly hard. Compared to older adults, they find negative information—the bad news—more memorable than positive information—or the good news. MRI studies show that twentysomething brains simply react more strongly to negative information than do the brains of older adults. There is more activity in the amygdala—the seat of the emotional brain.

When twentysomethings have their competence criticized, they become anxious and angry. They are tempted to march in and take action. They generate negative feelings toward others and obsess about the why: "Why did my boss say that? Why doesn't my boss like me?" Taking work so intensely personally can make a forty-hour workweek long indeed.

William James, the father of research psychology in the United States, said "The art of being wise is knowing what to overlook." Knowing what to overlook is one way that older adults *are* typically wiser than young adults. With age comes what is known as a positivity effect. We become more interested in positive information, and our brains react less strongly to what negative information we do encounter. We disengage with interpersonal conflict, choosing to let it be, especially when those in our network are involved.

I told Danielle how the twentysomething brain responds to surprise and criticism, how it makes many twentysomethings feel like, as one colleague says, leaves in the wind. A good day at work lifts us high in the air while a reprimand from a boss whips us down to the ground. As criticism blows us every which way, we feel—at work and in love—only as good as the last thing that happened.

"That's *exactly* how I feel," Danielle said. "Like a leaf. I never realized my boss would have this kind of effect. He's a bigger deal in my life right now than anybody. He's like God. Whatever he says seems like the ultimate judgment about me."

As we age, we feel less like leaves and more like trees. We

have roots that ground us and sturdy trunks that may sway, but don't break, in the wind. The wind that blows by can be more serious. "You're fired!" is much scarier when you have a mortgage. The things we do wrong at work are no longer typos but may be losing a $500,000 account or releasing software that crashes the company website for a day. But older adults—and even twentysomethings who work at it—can be rooted in the confidence that problems can be solved, or at least survived.

Sometimes my clients ask whether I ever lose sleep over work. Of course I do. Just last year I threw on a pair of jeans at midnight and sped to the emergency room after a client attempted suicide. I beat the ambulance there and as I stood in the wind in the hospital drive—and my clients' parents waited a thousand miles away for me to call with news—I was clear about one thing: As long as this young woman was alive, anything else could be gotten through. Getting through moments that are surprisingly hurtful or scary or sad was something that this client, who so fortunately did live, could not see for herself at that moment.

Danielle resisted quitting one week at a time. "I want to quit when I feel overwhelmed, like I have all this stuff that keeps coming and I keep getting it wrong," she said. "Like I'll have to work forever for these same people who see me as such a baby. It's like my back is up against the wall. I can't go home early or mess up when I'm here. I feel like I'm trapped forever with these awful feelings of anxiety and doubt. It's fight or flight all the time."

Twentysomethings and their active amygdalae often want to change their feelings by changing their jobs. They quit work that becomes messy or unpleasant, or they storm in and complain to their bosses' bosses, not realizing that their bosses' bosses' amygdalae are unlikely to be as worked up as their own. If Danielle left her job, she would feel better for a time. But quitting would also only confirm her fear: that she was a poseur who didn't belong in a good job anyway.

Danielle made up her mind to stay with her boss for at least one year, and she shifted to a different, also problematic, strategy: She started worrying all the time. Our sessions overflowed with errors she'd made, reasons she could be fired, or ways work could go wrong. Many days, she wandered the side streets during her lunch break and cried about the same things on the phone to her parents and her friends, only to turn around and head back into the building for more. Danielle knew these worries didn't actually prevent problems, but continuously imagining the worst did protect her from being caught off-guard when something did go wrong: "I'll do anything not to feel that awful Blitz feeling," she said.

Danielle's worries kept her from feeling surprised, but they did so by keeping her body in a chronically negatively aroused state. Sustained worrying drives the heart rate up. It raises levels of cortisol, or stress hormone. It leads to depressed thoughts.

Danielle said, "I think I've regressed. This is like when I had my first serious boyfriend in college and I constantly worried he was going to break up with me because he hated my outfit or something. I was always turning over in my mind everything he said and talking to all my girlfriends about it all the time. I had three or four friends on speed dial and we talked about it all the time."

"Do you know why it feels the same?"

"Because I'm dating my job and it's an abusive relationship?"

"No." I laughed. "Because it is the same. I have these same conversations with other twentysomething clients about their relationships. These clients worry incessantly about being dropped over some small thing. Or they get anxious when a few hours go by without an incoming text. Like you've been tempted to quit your job, they are tempted to break up or pick a fight to force some kind of closure so they don't get caught by surprise."

"I could *not* handle dating on top of all of this. What do you tell them?"

"The same thing I'm telling you. You have to get some roots and stand in the wind."

"So I just stuff all of my bad feelings and pretend they aren't happening?"

"No. Stuffing your feelings—that's not a root. That's no better than chronic worrying. Suppressing your feelings keeps your body and brain stressed, and it impairs your memory. It will leave you in sort of a fog."

"Then how do I calm down?"

Danielle said she felt trapped at work and trapped by her feelings of anxiety and doubt. This didn't have to be the case. Psychiatrist and Holocaust survivor Viktor Frankl describes our attitudes and reactions as being the last of our human freedoms. Danielle may not have had control over every situation at work, but she could control how she interpreted them and how she reacted to them. She could get out of her amygdala and put her frontal lobe to work.

Danielle needed to reappraise the meaning of her

difficult moments. When things went wrong on the job, Danielle immediately feared being fired and having to wait tables. This wasn't rational. Jobs—and relationships—usually aren't that fragile. Even if she did lose her job, I wasn't sure why she would be waiting tables as a result. Danielle needed to understand that tough days were just winds blowing by and that work was not as personal as she imagined it to be.

Reappraising lessens, and even prevents, bad feelings. If Danielle could reevaluate situations based on the facts, it would change not only how she dealt with work but also how she *felt* about it. Research shows that people who have some control over their emotions report greater life satisfaction, optimism, purpose, and better relationships with others.

"Right now, you're spending a lot of time hyping the emotions," I said. "To yourself and to other people on the phone. You're magnifying and catastrophizing every misstep. You've got to quit calling your mother on your lunch breaks."

"But calling my mom makes me feel better."

"I know it does. But those phone calls are robbing you of the opportunity to calm *yourself* down."

When Danielle called her mother, she was doing what psychologists call "borrowing an ego." She was reaching out in a moment of need and letting someone else's frontal lobe do the work. We all need to do that sometimes, but if we externalize our distress too much, we don't learn to handle bad days on our own. We don't practice soothing ourselves just when our brains are in the best position to pick up new skills. We don't learn how to calm ourselves down, and this in and of itself undermines confidence.

"What if you got yourself through your lunch hour?" I proposed to Danielle.

"I don't know how."

"Yes, you do. We've worked on this. You hang up the phone and you handle things."

"I handle things..."

"Yes. When something difficult happens at work, you can answer your emotional brain with reason. You think: 'What about the *facts*?'"

"The facts are that I look around at everybody else and I see I suck at my job," Danielle moped. "Maybe I don't have what it takes."

And so my own phone calls with Danielle continued.

Outside In

Inaction breeds fear and doubt. Action breeds confidence and courage. If you want to conquer fear, do not sit home and think about it. Go out and get busy.

—Dale Carnegie, writer and lecturer

Knowledge is not skill. Knowledge plus 10,000 times is skill.

—Shinichi Suzuki, founder of the Suzuki Method for music instruction

"Maybe you don't have what it takes," I repeated to Danielle. "What does that even mean?"

"In television, you always hear about how people have *it*. One day I asked my boss if he thought I had it, and you know what he said? He said, 'No, you don't have it, but if you work hard you could.' "

"How did you interpret that?" I asked.

"It sort of made me feel good, like I wasn't doing all this

for nothing, but it also made me feel second-rate, like I'm not a natural in his eyes."

"A natural," I said back.

"Yeah."

"What's *it* anyway? What do you imagine everybody else just has that you don't?" I asked.

"Confidence," Danielle answered simply.

"Why *would* you have confidence?" I asked. "You just started your career."

Danielle looked at some of her coworkers and was just sure they were born with self-assurance, or at least graduated with it, when, in fact, most of the people she compared herself to were older than she was or had been working longer than she had. She imagined that people at work either had confidence or they didn't, so any little thing that went wrong on the job suggested she didn't. Her mistakes became statements about *who she was*, perhaps a person not assured enough for a career in television, and not just feedback about what she needed to learn or a reflection of where she was in her career: the beginning. She feared every reprimand indicated she was not a natural, and this left her devastated. It sometimes made quitting seem like her only option.

Danielle's idea that people were innately confident on the job, or they weren't, is called a fixed mindset. We can have fixed mindsets about different things—intelligence, athletic ability, social savvy, thinness—but, whatever the case, a fixed mindset is a way of thinking in black and white. When it came to confidence, Danielle thought there were haves and have-nots and maybe she was a have-not. She feared her more self-possessed coworkers were cut out for the work when she obviously wasn't. This made work a scary place. Big mistakes or negative comments felt like verdicts.

Those who use what is called a growth mindset believe that people can change, that success is something to be achieved. Maybe it's not the case that any person can be anything, but it is still true that within certain parameters, people can learn and grow. For those who have a growth mindset, failures may sting but they are also viewed as opportunities for improvement and change.

Decades of research in schools tells us that a fixed mindset gets in the way of success. Schoolkids with fixed mindsets enjoy work that affirms their belief that they have *it*—whether the *it* is science smarts or talent on the basketball court. But once the work becomes challenging, these same kids stop enjoying school. They feel threatened by hard work, fearing it means they don't have *it* after all. Struggle means being a have-not.

Consider this.

In a longitudinal study of college students, freshmen were evaluated for fixed mindsets or growth mindsets and then followed across their four years of enrollment. When the students with fixed mindsets encountered academic challenges such as daunting projects or low grades, they gave up, while the students with growth mindsets responded by working harder or trying new strategies. Rather than strengthening their skills and toughening their resolve, four years of college left the students with fixed mindsets feeling less confident. The feelings they most associated with school were distress, shame, and upset. Those with growth mindsets performed better in school overall and, at graduation time, they reported feeling confident, determined, enthusiastic, inspired, and strong.

Outside In

As it goes for students, twentysomethings' theories about success and confidence can have a profound effect on their performance on the job. Danielle was a hard worker who'd clearly had a growth mindset when she was in college. That's how she wound up in her high-profile job. But somehow Danielle had the wrong ideas about work.

While some research suggests that individuals strongly hold either a fixed mindset or a growth one when it comes to qualities such as intelligence, to assume that Danielle was a have-not when it came to a growth mindset would be premature. I suspected Danielle believed that people at work either had what it took or they didn't, not because she had a permanently fixed mindset about confidence but because she didn't understand the workplace. If Danielle learned more about where on-the-job confidence actually came from, how she saw herself could change.

Confidence doesn't come from the inside out. It moves from the outside in. People feel less anxious—and more confident—on the inside when they can point to things they have done well on the outside. Fake confidence comes from stuffing our self-doubt. Empty confidence comes from parental platitudes on our lunch hour. Real confidence comes from mastery experiences, which are actual, lived moments of success, especially when things seem difficult. Whether we are talking about love or work, the confidence that overrides insecurity comes from experience. There is no other way.

It is not uncommon for twentysomething clients to come to therapy hoping I can help them increase their confidence. Some wonder if maybe I do hypnosis and a hypnotherapy session might do the trick (I don't, and it wouldn't), or they hope I can recommend some herbal remedy (I can't). The way I help twentysomethings gain confidence is by sending them back to work or back to their relationships with some better information. I teach them about how they can have more mastery over their emotions. I talk to them about what confidence really is.

Literally, confidence means "with trust." In research psychology, the more precise term is self-efficacy, or one's ability to be effective or produce the desired result. No matter what word you use, confidence is trusting yourself to get the job done—whether that job is public speaking, sales, teaching, or being an assistant—and that trust only comes from having *gotten* the job done many times before. As was the case for every other twentysomething I'd worked with, Danielle's confidence on the job could only come from doing well on the job—but not all the time.

Sometimes Danielle fantasized about "waiting tables or working in some easy job where [she] didn't have to think or didn't make mistakes." But twentysomethings who hide out in underemployment, especially those who are hiding out because of a lack of confidence, are not serving themselves.

For work success to lead to confidence, the job has to be challenging and it must require effort. It has to be done without too much help. And it cannot go well every single day. A long run of easy successes creates a sort of fragile confidence, the kind that is shattered when the first failure comes along. A more resilient confidence comes from succeeding—and from surviving some failures.

"I spend most of my days at work managing how I feel," Danielle complained. "Sometimes it's all I can do not to lash out at someone. It's all I can do just to stay in the building for the whole day."

"*That's* a mastery experience. Mastering your emotions at work builds confidence. Then you can hang around long enough to have other successes at work. It's going to take time. You need more mastery experiences."

"Like how many more, exactly?" Danielle asked.

"There is no magic number," I said.

"Can you give me an estimate?" she continued, only partially kidding.

"OK. About ten thousand hours' worth."

"*Ugh!*" Danielle shouted into the phone. "Where did you get *that*?"

I told Danielle about the work of K. Anders Ericsson, a research psychologist who is probably the expert on, well, expertise. In years of study, he and his colleagues have looked at surgeons, pianists, writers, investors, darts players, violinists, and other types of talent. They have found that a large part of what makes people good—and even great—at what they do is time in. For the most part, "naturals" are myths. People who are especially good at something may have some innate inclination, or some particular talent, but they have *also* spent about ten thousand hours practicing or doing that thing.

Not everyone wants to be a virtuoso, but most twentysomethings I know want to be exceptionally good at what they choose to do. In most cases, it is going to take at least ten thousand hours of their time. Sometimes it seems that the challenge of the twentysomething years is to figure out what to do, and then suddenly it will just start happening. We imagine we will show up at work and instantly add value or be taken seriously. This is not the case. Knowing you *want* to do something isn't the same as knowing *how* to do it, and even knowing *how* to do something isn't the same as actually *doing it well.*

The real challenge of the twentysomething years is the work itself. Ten thousand hours is five years of focused, full-time work (40 hours × 50 work weeks a year = 2,000 hours a year × 5 years = 10,000 hours) or ten years of less-targeted work (20 hours × 50 work weeks a year = 1,000 hours a year × 10 years = 10,000 hours). My ten thousand hours were seven years of graduate school. Danielle's ten thousand hours were going to be five to ten years of working her way up and around in producing. That's why she needed to dig in now.

"Oh my *God*," Danielle said. "I don't think I can work for my crazy boss for five years. *For ten thousand hours?*"

"It may not all be at the same job. Besides, you're not at zero."

Danielle was giving away some of her confidence by not recognizing the successes she had already earned. She'd been performing well at a difficult job for six months, so she had done about a thousand hours so far. She also had hundreds of hours of experience from previous internships. It was time to take stock of what she had.

She made a list of the relevant things she'd mastered in school and at work. She hung up her diploma in her apartment. She started taking herself seriously by dressing more professionally. She stopped calling her parents and her friends on her lunch hour so she could give herself credit for getting through the day. She cleaned up the way she talked about herself on the job: "No more self-deprecating stories," she declared.

Danielle had been avoiding feedback at work because she felt almost terrorized by comments that had come her way. This was not working in her favor. Without concrete information, Danielle was too quick to assume the worst. Positive feedback would give her the opportunity to feel better, and negative feedback would give her the chance to do better.

Danielle made it through her first year on the job. After much urging during our Monday-morning sessions, she requested a one-year performance review at work. Her typically harried and unforgiving boss slowed down long enough to read the paperwork aloud. He had written that Danielle was "the best assistant" he'd had in a long time, a "hard worker who came in on Saturdays to produce her own stories," a "a go-getter," and a "calm problem solver." (Ha! she said about that last one.) Danielle received a thousand-dollar year-end bonus and decided that the bonus was worth an extra thousand hours toward the total ten thousand hours.

"Fair enough," I said.

With every week, work was a bit less dramatic. When things went wrong, which they still did all the time, Danielle didn't feel as judged. She realized that there was a difference between having a feeling and acting on it. Now when she felt anxious or incompetent, she calmed herself with what had gone well.

Around this time, my phone sessions with Danielle stopped being about quitting her job. Her amygdala was quieting down. Her frontal lobe was working hard. She handled new problems with less emotion and more reason.

By our estimate, Danielle had about six thousand hours to go before she would probably feel confident at work. She still worried on Sunday nights when faced with another week, but her boss seemed less awful and Danielle knew she should stay at her job at least until she found something better. A year or so later, she received an e-mail from another assistant across town:

"There's an awesome job over here with the president of production. You should jump on this because you'd get to produce all the time. There is no one here we like for it so we will definitely be posting the job. Get in here before that. P.S. The guy you'd work for is nice!"

Danielle got the new job and faced quitting her old one. "Looks like I'm going to be working toward my ten thousand hours elsewhere!"

"Terrific," I said.

"So what are we going to talk about now?" she asked.

"What about relationships? Last year, you said you couldn't handle dating."

"Oy," Danielle said quickly. "I want a relationship in theory. But I still cannot imagine having the time to meet anybody, much less figuring out how to be in a relationship. Can I deal with that way, *way* later?"

"A little bit later," I said. "You can go to work and be in love at the same time, you know. In fact, it would be good for you."

Getting Along and Getting Ahead

Life itself still remains a very effective therapist.

—Karen Horney, psychoanalyst

Love and work are the cornerstones of our humanness.

—Sigmund Freud, neurologist and founder of psychoanalysis

For many years, there has been a spirited debate among personality researchers about whether people change after age thirty. Numerous studies have shown that, relatively speaking, we don't. After thirty, our thoughts and feelings and behaviors remain incredibly stable. Those who are relatively extraverted keep being relatively extraverted, and those who are conscientious keep being conscientious.

But there is still some disagreement about exactly how much people don't change. One side says "Barring interventions or catastrophic events, personality traits appear to be essentially fixed after age thirty." The other side is more optimistic, holding out for some change albeit "small in magnitude." Whether, after thirty, we can expect to change a bit or not at all, what all sides of the post-thirty debate have recently come to agree on is something that many clinicians have known all along: Our personalities change more during the twentysomething years *than at any time before or after.*

This is big news because conventional wisdom tells us that childhood or adolescence is when our personalities are on the move. There's the Jesuit maxim "Give me the child until he is seven and I'll give you the man." Freud's theory of personality development ended at puberty. And in the media, adolescence is portrayed as our one opportunity to try being someone new.

We now know that, of any time in life, our twenties are our best chance for change. I have seen twentysomethings move from socially anxious to socially confident-enough, or get beyond years of childhood unhappiness, in a relatively short period of time. And because these changes are happening just as long-term careers and relationships are being decided, these same shifts can lead to very different lives. The twenties are a time when people and personalities are poised for transformation.

I once supervised a psychology graduate student who told me she disliked working with twentysomethings. She said when she worked with older adults in therapy she felt like a medical examiner, like her job was to figure out what had gone wrong in people's lives and to bring closure. She imagined she was investigating a death of sorts, finding problems that led to divorce or career failure or some other personal demise.

When she worked with twentysomethings, this graduate

student said she felt more pressure. She worried she might make them better—or worse. She said she felt like there was "more on the table." This student may not have fully understood therapy with older adults, but she was right about one thing: The twentysomething years are no time for a postmortem. Life isn't over. It is not too late.

Sam found out over a bowl of Cheerios that his parents were divorcing. On that particular Saturday morning, he was twelve years old, and it was two weeks before the seventh grade would begin.

Sam's mother told him she'd bought a house down the street. Life would go on the same as before, only in two homes, she promised. She cheerily recruited Sam to help her move out and, to a kid his age, carting boxes to a new place seemed exciting and neat. Now with great insight, he said, "My mom let me be too helpful. She let me enjoy it too much." Sam felt conned.

Each of Sam's parents wanted to be part of his day-to-day life, so when the school year began, he switched houses every day. In the morning he packed the clothes and books he thought he would need for that day and part of the next. He'd wake up the next morning and do it all again. For the next six years, the only constant was worrying about what he had left behind or feeling mad about what he was hauling around. To Sam, the "every-other-night shit" had been in his parents' best interests, not his own. It had been a way for Sam's parents to deny that their lives *were* changing and that everyone was going to miss out—most of all Sam.

After many sessions spent talking about Sam's parents' divorce, I started to feel stressed. I noticed I sometimes wanted to say, "Move on!" This was an unsympathetic urge, especially because what Sam had to say was important. Upon giving it some thought, I realized the impulse probably came from my not knowing much about Sam's current life.

Sam had come to therapy because, ever since his parents' divorce, he'd felt "anxious and angry." Eventually he was going to expect to feel better, and I knew talking about the past was only going to get us so far. I made a conscious effort to direct our attention to Sam's present, which I found was not going well.

Every time I'd seen Sam, he had a backpack. I now learned the backpack usually had clothes and maybe a toothbrush in it because Sam never knew when he would make it home, or where exactly home was. Sam said he lived in about five different places. Technically, he resided with his mother and stepfather. But he often crashed at friends' apartments, especially if, after a late night out, it was easier to stay on that side of town.

Sam's résumé was as scattered as the various places he slept. He'd changed jobs nearly every year since college. Currently, he was "funemployed," which meant he was supposed to be enjoying himself and riding out unemployment benefits, but life was becoming less and less fun. He bemoaned living life "at loose ends." He no longer enjoyed going out like he used to. He so anxiously anticipated the question of "What do you do?" that he'd taken to having a couple of shots of liquor before leaving the house on Friday or Saturday evenings. Whenever the conversations at parties turned to jobs, Sam felt self-conscious, and he headed off to get a stronger drink.

"It's weird," Sam said. "The older I get, the less I feel like a man."

"I'm not sure you're giving yourself much to feel like a man about," I offered.

From what I could see, Sam still lived like a vagrant. Switching jobs and houses, he was keeping on with the "every-other-night shit" of his childhood in a twentysomething way. No wonder he was anxious and angry. No wonder he didn't feel like a man.

I told Sam I was glad he'd come to therapy. It made sense for us to spend some time talking about his parents' split and about how this led to living out of a backpack. I also told him he didn't have to live out of a backpack anymore. In fact, as long as he kept it up, he was going to keep feeling the same.

"Things are totally hopeless. I can't change," Sam said to me one day as he leaned over, elbows on his knees and rubbing his head all over like he'd come straight from getting a really short haircut. "I need a brain transplant."

"Your brain does get used to doing things a certain way. But I don't feel hopeless about you at all. I feel quite hopeful."

"*Why?*" he asked, with a sort of helpless sarcasm that captured the anger and the anxiety he'd described.

"Because you're in your twenties. Your brain can change. Your personality can change."

"How?" he wondered aloud, this time with a touch more curiosity than cynicism.

"That brain transplant you want, it's going to come from a life transplant. By joining the world, you could feel a lot better."

Sam and I talked about a Pew Research Center study showing that, contrary to what movies and blogs may lead us to believe, employed twentysomethings are happier than unemployed twentysomethings. I suggested that, in addition to therapy, Sam get a job and, while he was at it, a regular place to sleep. The cynicism quickly returned, with Sam saying some boring job would only make him feel worse. Being responsible for an apartment would just add to the things he was always forgetting to do. A steady job and a place to take care of were the last things he needed, he said.

Sam was wrong.

Numerous studies from around the world show that life starts to feel better across the twentysomething years. We become more emotionally stable and less tossed around by life's ups and downs. We become more conscientious and responsible. We become more socially competent. We feel more agreeable about life and more able to cooperate with others. Overall, we become happier and more confident and less—as Sam put it—anxious and angry. But these sorts of changes don't happen for everyone. Sam couldn't keep walking around with his backpack, waiting to feel better.

In our twenties, positive personality changes come from what researchers call "getting along and getting ahead." Feeling better doesn't come from avoiding adulthood, it comes from investing in adulthood. These are the years when we move from school to work, from hookups to relationships or, in Sam's case, from couches to apartments. Most of these changes are about making adult commitments—to bosses, partners, leases, roommates—and these commitments shift how we are in the world and who we are inside.

The investments we make in work and love trigger personality maturation. Being a cooperative colleague or a successful partner is what drives personality change. Settling down simply helps us feel more settled. Twentysomethings who don't feel like they are getting along or getting ahead, on the other hand, feel stressed and angry and alienated—like Sam.

There are all sorts of ways to make commitments to the world around us and, sometimes, in our twenties we have to be forgiving about what being settled or successful means. A great relationship or a job to be proud of may seem elusive, but just working *toward* these things makes us happier. Twentysomethings who experience even some workplace success or financial security are more confident, positive, and responsible than those who do not.

Even simply having goals can make us happier and more confident—both now and later. In one study that followed nearly five hundred young adults from college to the mid-thirties, increased goal-setting in the twenties led to greater purpose, mastery, agency, and well-being in the thirties. Goals are how we declare who we are and who we want to be. They are how we structure our years and our lives. Goals have been called the building blocks of adult personality, and it is worth considering that who you will be in your thirties and beyond is being built out of the goals you are setting for yourself today.

Outside of work, commitments to others also foster change and well-being. Studies in the United States and Europe have found that entering into stable relationships helps twentysomethings feel more secure and responsible, whether these relationships last or not. Steady relationships reduce social anxiety and depression as they help us feel less lonely and give us the opportunity to practice our interpersonal skills. We learn about managing our emotions and about conflict resolution. As we take part in partnering, we find new ways to feel competent in the adult world. And on the days we do feel bad about our twenties, these relationships can be a source of security and a more mature safe haven than what we have with our parents.

Being single while you're young may be glorified in the press, but staying single across the twenties does not typically feel good. A study that tracked men and women from their early twenties to their later twenties found that of those who remained single—who dated or hooked up but avoided commitments—80 percent were dissatisfied with their dating lives and only 10 percent didn't wish they had a partner. Being chronically uncoupled may be especially detrimental to men, as those who remained single throughout their twenties experienced a significant dip in their self-esteem near thirty.

Sam had it all backward. The way he saw it, he couldn't join the world until he felt like a man, but he wasn't going to feel like a man until he joined the world. Sam imagined that the real world would just add to his problems, but if he wanted to feel less anxious and angry in his twenties—or his thirties—setting goals and making commitments was the proven way to go.

Sam started to look for an apartment. At first, he would only commit to a series of short sublets. He felt calmer for months at a time, but then the backpack would reappear. Sam didn't see any good reason to have an apartment—until he realized what he most wanted was a dog.

He felt almost too ashamed to tell me he'd once had a dog, before his parents divorced. After the split, it became unclear who was supposed to be taking care of the dog. The dog stopped being attended to and started having behavior problems, like chewing through rugs or growling at people. Before long, the dog was given away. Sam blamed himself for not having done better by his dog. I tried to reassure Sam that what happened to his dog—and to him—was his parents' failing, not his own. I could see that talking about it was almost unbearable for him.

When Sam got an apartment and a dog, he came to life. Caring for the dog and walking the dog gave Sam the rhythm and meaning that had been missing for years. He would tell funny stories about his dog and show me pictures. I could almost see his personality—and his life—shifting from across the room. Sam started walking dogs for money. He worked as an assistant to an obedience coach. He soon saved up enough to start his own small business: a canine day care called Dog Days. This was, Sam said, his chance to do it differently.

Not long after Dog Days got going, Sam stopped therapy. It was difficult for him to meet regularly, because he needed to be at work. A couple of years later, Sam e-mailed to say that he felt happier and more confident. He was in the same apartment. He was renting a big warehouse space for Dog Days, and had a business plan that included expanding into another space on the other side of town. He was in a serious relationship and was volunteering as a puppy raiser for guide dogs.

Sam said he wasn't ready for marriage yet but he'd been thinking more about being a parent. He'd been mad at his own parents for so long—and he'd let them take care of him for so long—he had forgotten to notice that caring for someone or something was a real strength of his own. He was good at it, and it made him feel good in return. Being a dad was something he knew he didn't want to miss.

Every Body

The management of fertility is one of the most important functions of adulthood.

—Germaine Greer, feminist theorist

There was a fair amount of media buzz when Demi Moore, age forty-seven, said she wanted to have a baby with her then-husband, Ashton Kutcher, age thirty-two. In a May 2010 interview with UK *Elle* magazine, Ms. Moore said, "We talk about it and it's something we would like. He's an amazing father to my daughters already, so I have no doubt that if it's in our future, it would be an incredible part of our journey together."

From the article, it's not clear whether Ms. Moore meant that the couple wanted to adopt or use an egg donor or have a baby the old-fashioned way. But the headlines flew: DEMI MOORE WANTS TO HAVE A BABY WITH ASHTON KUTCHER; DEMI MOORE AND ASHTON KUTCHER HOPE FOR A BABY; ASHTON

KUTCHER TALKS BIOLOGICAL BABIES WITH DEMI MOORE. These headlines troubled me. I envisioned young women everywhere imagining that Ms. Moore was pushing the boundaries for their biological clocks just as she has for how great women can look after forty. Unfortunately, it is not that simple.

As the average life expectancy increases and young adults marry later and spend more time on education and work, more couples are having their first child in their thirties and even forties. A 2010 report by the Pew Research Center titled "The New Demography of American Motherhood" shows that today's mother is older and more educated than the mothers of the past. Babies born to mothers over thirty-five now outnumber those born to teen moms, and the average age for first-time motherhood is twenty-five, with about one-third of first-time moms over thirty. The number of women who opt for childbearing between the ages of thirty-five and thirty-nine has increased by nearly 50 percent in the last twenty years, and by 80 percent for women aged forty to forty-four.

For many, it just isn't feasible to have children before work and love are figured out, and research consistently shows that educated moms are on the rise and good for kids. And, for the first time in history, women outnumber men in the workplace, which means that more women—and men—are balancing work and family. None of this has changed the way our bodies work. It has just changed how much we need to know about fertility.

Fertility might sound like a topic for a thirtysomething or fortysomething book, but it's not. In a different Pew survey, when twentysomethings were asked to identify their top priorities, the majority—52 percent—named being a good parent as one of the most important goals in life. Next in line was having a successful marriage at 30 percent. Compare this to the 15 percent who prioritized a high-paying career, the 9 percent who most valued free time, and the 1 percent who hoped to become famous.

These numbers tell us that what many twentysomethings most want is to have happy families, at least eventually. These twentysomethings have a right to know that the years just ahead are their most fertile. They deserve to be educated about fertility statistics before they themselves *are* the statistics.

What is about to follow are some sobering statistics about having babies after the age of thirty-five. Medicine has been called "a science of uncertainty and an art of probability," and this holds especially true for reproductive medicine. It is an imperfect science, so not all pre-thirty-five women will easily have the babies they want, nor is it true that those over thirty-five will not. But there are some age-related changes that everyone who wants children would be better off understanding.

Most of these changes are about female fertility, because this is something scientists know a lot about. Still, a biological clock ticks in both women and men. Researchers are beginning to find that older sperm may be associated with various neurocognitive problems in children, including autism, schizophrenia, dyslexia, and lower intelligence. For this reason, and for reasons we will discuss further into the chapter, both men and women ought to be thinking about the timing of babies.

To be transparent, I had both of my children in my

thirties—at thirty-five and thirty-seven to be exact. Like many twentysomethings, I wanted to establish my career before I had kids, and I did. I waddled across the stage to collect my PhD diploma while eight months pregnant with baby number one. Before baby number two, I had a private practice and a university job. I've learned a lot about fertility since then—mine, my clients', and women's in general. Having two babies after thirty-five did not go quite as smoothly as I expected, and now I see how lucky I was. Many women are not as fortunate. Women like Kaitlyn.

Kaitlyn was thirty-four when she met Ben. They had been dating for two years when she came to my office to talk about transitioning to marriage. Marriage, a first for each, was "definitely" in the future. Kaitlyn talked about a wedding a lot but never mentioned children. I was tempted to assume she did not want them. I decided to ask instead. "What about kids?" I queried.

Kaitlyn seemed taken aback. "I don't know. I haven't decided that yet."

Her response made me annoyed, not at Kaitlyn, but at a culture that has told women that the decision about whether to have a baby is something that, even at thirty-six, is not pressing. I thought about a recent article I'd read in which a woman talked about feeling misled into thinking she would succeed at pregnancy as long as she got started "by the time [she] was thirty-eight or forty." Katilyn seemed to think that too.

"Then now is the time to decide," I said. "You don't want to figure out children are important to you just when you can no longer have them."

"What good would it do right now? I'm not even married...."

"You could be, easily. Or you could have a baby first. Getting married is a cinch, but having kids may not be."

"But I want the big wedding that all my friends got to have. I want the dress and the pictures. Do you know how many weddings I've been to—*stag*? How many presents I've bought? I'm guessing we won't be through an engagement and a wedding for at least a couple of years. Then it would be nice to have a couple of years together without kids first."

"All those things would be nice. I know marriage has been a long time coming and a big wedding would be really special. I still want you to make sure a child isn't something you might want to prioritize even more."

Now Kaitlyn seemed annoyed with me. "People have kids in their forties," she said. "It is way more common than it used to be. I have two forty-year-old friends who just had babies. People in Hollywood do it all the time."

"More women do than in the past, that's true," I said. "But so many women *can't*. We do hear about this or that Hollywood fortysomething woman who is having a baby. But if you look a bit closer, you'll often find out about the half-dozen fertility treatments that went into it. Or you see the statistics about the everyday fortysomething women who wanted to have kids but couldn't. That doesn't make the headlines."

Kaitlyn was relying on a reasoning error known as the availability heuristic. The availability heuristic is a mental shortcut whereby we decide how likely something is based on how easy it is to bring an example to mind. Kaitlyn was right that it is more common than it used to be for older women to have babies. She personally knew two forty-year-old women who had succeeded, and she could think of lots of famous women who had as well. But she did not know the statistics about how easy it is—and is not—to have kids as we approach our forties. Kaitlyn didn't know the facts.

Fertility, or the ability to reproduce, peaks for women during the late twentysomething years. Biologically speaking, the twenties will be the easiest time to have a baby for most women. Some declines in fertility begin at about thirty and at thirty-five, a woman's ability to become pregnant and carry a baby to term drops considerably. At forty, fertility plummets.

This is because of two age-related changes that every woman can expect across her thirties and forties: Egg quality decreases and the endocrine system, which regulates hormones and tells the body how to proceed with a pregnancy, becomes less effective. With these changes, pregnancy becomes less likely and miscarriage becomes more likely. Lower-quality eggs have trouble implanting and maturing. Even good eggs can be derailed by hormones gone awry.

Compared to their twentysomething selves, women are about half as fertile at thirty, about one-quarter as fertile at thirty-five, and about one-eighth as fertile at forty. That's one reason why, if we look at the actual base rates for babies born in the United States in 2007, about one million babies were born to mothers aged twenty to twenty-four, another million were born to mothers aged twenty-five to twenty-nine, just under one million were born to mothers aged thirty to thirty-four, about half a million babies were born to mothers aged thirty-five to thirty-nine, only about 100,000 were born to mothers aged forty to forty-four, and fewer than 10,000 were born to women forty-five and over.

Kaitlyn's big wedding came and went and, at thirty-eight, she began to try to get pregnant. It did not go well. After a year of trying and two miscarriages, she and her husband were referred to a fertility specialist. Kaitlyn was sure that with the proper treatment she would have a baby soon.

The first signs of decreased fertility are difficulty becoming and staying pregnant. Trying au natural—just having sex around the time of ovulation—a woman has about a 20 to 25 percent chance of conceiving during each cycle, up to about age thirty-five. So when you're young it takes, on average, about four or five months of having sex to get pregnant. After thirty-five, the per-cycle odds of pregnancy start to drop sharply, down to 5 percent at forty, then 3 percent at forty-one, and 2 percent at forty-two. At forty, that's an average of twenty or more months of trying, and the longer we have to spend trying, the worse our odds become. Add to this the rising rates of miscarriage in women over thirty-five—one-quarter of pregnancies after thirty-five and half of pregnancies after forty miscarry—and the post-thirty-five years can be a time of anticipation and heartbreak for couples like Kaitlyn and Ben.

When couples try to get pregnant but can't, many like Kaitlyn and Ben turn to fertility treatments, hoping for a remedy. Sometimes it works, and that we hear about. More often it does not, and that we may not hear about.

One indicator of how difficult it can be to have a baby as we age is the cost. The average cost of a fertility intervention for a twentysomething couple is $25,000. By thirty-five, the cost is about $35,000. After age 35, as the obstacles to pregnancy increase, so does the price tag. At forty, couples who need fertility treatments will pay an average of $100,000 for one live birth. By age forty-two, the average cost goes up to about $300,000 for a baby.

Even if money isn't an obstacle, nature may still be. Fertility treatments fail more than they succeed. Past age thirty-five, intrauterine insemination—or the "turkey baster method" in which sperm is inserted into the female reproductive tract—has a 90 to 95 percent *failure* rate. In vitro fertilization—"IVF" or "in vitro," when sperm and egg are united outside the body and implanted in the uterus—succeeds only about 10 to 20 percent of the time. In older women, the failure rate for these procedures is so high, many fertility clinics will not perform them on fortysomething women at all. The failed attempts bring down the success rates the clinics are able to advertise.

Sadly, Kaitlyn and Ben never had a baby. Kaitlyn tried intrauterine insemination, a few rounds of IVF, and hormone treatments, but none were successful. By forty-three, clinics were no longer willing to treat her. Doctors suggested egg donation or adoption but, for the time being, Ben and Kaitlyn felt too physically and financially exhausted to go forward. After working with Kaitlyn as she scoured the Internet, first for wedding venues and then for a way to have a baby, our sessions were now about grief.

In 1970, one in ten fortysomething women were childless. Today, one in five are. It's true that more women and men are childless by choice. Being a parent is nothing to be idealized. As meaningful as it can be, it is also unrelenting hard work. It can be an emotional stretch. So some couples opt out of parenthood in order to focus on work or other pursuits.

But according to a National Survey of Family Growth, about half of childless couples are *not* childless by choice. They are like Kaitlyn and Ben. They are thirtysomething and fortysomething women and men who feel they did not consider the facts about fertility soon enough, like maybe when they were twentysomethings who, even if they weren't ready to have children, could have planned work and family trajectories with different outcomes.

Fertility may seem like a women's issue, but as more couples have their first child in their thirties and forties, timing affects everybody. Not included in the statistics above are the countless men and women, straight and gay, who did have children in their thirties and forties but who were surprised by how difficult the process turned out to be. What fertility specialists don't hear about—and psychologists do—is how modern marriages and partnerships are affected by later childbearing and child rearing.

It affects women *and men* when ovulation kits come on the honeymoon and sex becomes a calendar-driven quest for a baby. Many couples suffer through multiple rounds of fertility treatments, shrouding marriage, pregnancy, and even babyhood in anxiety and stress. Lesbian couples and single women who want biological children will likely face some "fertility" intervention, and these become trickier and costlier the later they occur. Too many men and women grieve not having all the children they want, or not being able to give their child a sibling, as they find that, because of their twentysomething choices, they have now run out of time.

Even if we assume couples will have all the children they hope for with no trouble whatsoever, a 2010 study shows that simply postponing marriage and children leads to more stressful lives for families. When babies need to come so quickly and so close together after "I do," newlywed couples are thrust directly into what research shows are typically the most strained years of marriage. This is especially true as the work of raising young children collides with our peak earning years.

According to the parents surveyed, about half feel they have too little time with their youngest child, about two-thirds feel they have too little time with their spouse, and another two-thirds report too little time for themselves. An article discussing this study factored in yet another wrinkle, saying, "Many men and women feel hugely stretched and stressed trying to help out their not fully independent twentysomething children at the same time the health of their octogenarian parents is failing."

"*Twentysomething* children?" I thought as I read the article.

Being whipsawed by the needs of a twentysomething child in college and a parent in a nursing home may be the case for many today, barely one generation into the widespread delay of marriage and kids. But this is a shortsighted analysis. If you have your kids between thirty-five and forty and they have their kids between thirty-five and forty, in one more generation it will be quite common, especially among the well-educated who tend to postpone childbearing the longest, for parents to be pulled in two directions not by twentysomethings and octogenarians but by *toddlers and octogenarians*. Men and women will soon face caring for two entirely dependent groups of loved ones at precisely the moment they are most needed back at work.

It changes things when Grandma and Grandpa aren't

up to babysitting, and when they can't handle the kids for a couples' weekend away. But this says nothing of the less quantifiable—and more poignant—effects of longer spaces between generations. There is something profoundly sad about seeing an eighty-year-old grandmother come to the hospital to meet a grandchild. It is crushing to realize there won't be many sunny days at the lake with Grandpa or holidays spent in Grandma's loving presence. It feels almost wrong to look at our children and wonder how long they will have their grandparents in their lives—or even how long they will have us.

The best way I know to explain this is to talk about Billy. Billy is not an outlier. He is a smart, college-educated man who'd heard his twenties were his last chance for fun and adventure, the goal being to gather "few regrets and a million memories." That's not quite how it ended up. Billy had a lot of regrets about his twentysomething pursuits, which only later did he realize were not as important, or even as memorable, as he once thought.

I worked with Billy in his midthirties, as he married, had a son, and turned more seriously toward work. It was stressful, trying to do everything at once. He often felt his job and his family needed more attention than he could give. One day at the office, he had such chest and head pains he called his wife to drive him to the hospital. The next day, he underwent an MRI, which fortunately turned up nothing serious, except his own personal reckoning.

In our next session, I said nothing as he spoke. The hour went by, him talking, me listening. I was so moved by his experience, I didn't dare interrupt him. I wished twentysomethings everywhere could have heard what Billy said. I want Billy to have the last word on this:

> So I went for my MRI and it was a really fucking scary thing. Being cooped up in that magnet coffin with all that whirring and banging. There was an alarm sound that kept going off. The machine was the only thing in this big sterile room, and the operator sat in a booth on the other side of the wall. It was seven thirty in the morning and really cold. They gave me headphones with music to drown out some of the noise, and it was on a preset station. Ozzy Osbourne was playing, believe it or not. There was a time when that would have been funny to me. But it was just ironic or pathetic. Nothing could have felt more irrelevant to my life at that moment than Ozzy Osbourne. I was really scared of what they were going to find.
>
> And the funny—no, *sad*—thing was my life didn't flash before my eyes. Not at all. I'm thirty-eight years old and there were, like, two things I had in my mind—the way my little son's hand feels when I hold it and how I didn't want to leave my wife behind to do it all on her own. What seemed plain to me was that I wasn't scared of losing my past. I was scared of losing my future. I felt like almost nothing in my life mattered up until just a few years ago. I realized that all the good stuff is still to come. I was so sick and panicked that I might never see my son ride a bike,

play soccer, graduate from school, get married, have his own kids. And my career was just getting good.

Nothing is wrong, thank God. But this has made me face some things. I saw my regular doctor a couple of days after the MRI, and I told her she needed to keep me going for a good twenty years at least. She said she sees that a lot now. When people had their kids at twenty-two, it was pretty much a given you'd be around to finish what you started. Nobody worried about it. Now she says a lot of parents come in and say, "Hey, I need to be healthy at least until my kids are off in college. *Please* be sure I make it that long." How screwed up is that?

What I can't figure out, and what I feel like I am grieving a little, is why I spent so many years on nothing. So many years doing things and hanging out with people that don't even rate a memory. For what? I had a good time in my twenties, but did I need to do all that *for eight years*? Lying there in the MRI, it was like I traded five years of partying or hanging out in coffee shops for five more years I could have had with my son if I'd grown up sooner. Why didn't someone drop the manners and tell me I was wasting my life?

Do the Math

Be ruled by time, the wisest counselor of all.

—Plutarch, historian

To achieve great things, two things are needed: a plan, and not quite enough time.

—Leonard Bernstein, composer

In 1962, a twenty-three-year-old French speleologist named Michel Siffre spent two months in a cave. Siffre wanted to live beyond time, isolated from changes in light, sound, and temperature. He was interested in how people understand time in the absence of obvious markers. When Siffre emerged, he thought he had been underground only twenty-five days, about half as long as he actually had. Siffre had lost track of time. Decades and several similar studies later, we now know that the brain has difficulty keeping time across long, unpunctuated intervals. We condense unmarked time.

The days and years pass, and we say, "Where did the time go?"

Our twenties can be like living beyond time. When we graduate from school, we leave behind the only lives we have ever known, ones that have been neatly packaged in semester-sized chunks with goals nestled within. Suddenly, life opens up and the syllabi are gone. There are days and weeks and months and years, but no clear way to know when or why any one thing should happen. It can be a disorienting, cavelike existence. As one twentysomething astutely put it, "The twentysomething years are a whole new way of thinking about time. There's this big chunk of time and a whole bunch of stuff needs to happen somehow."

Laura Carstensen is a researcher at Stanford University who studies time. When Carstensen was twenty-one, a car accident left her hospitalized for many months. During her hospital stay, she started to think about how both young and old people perceive their time left on earth. These reflections led to a career spent studying how we think about age and time, and how this may influence the lives we lead.

In one recent project, Carstensen has worked with twentysomethings to understand better why people do or don't save for retirement. Now, I can honestly say that in all my hours of work with twentysomethings, retirement planning has almost never come up. Saving money in our twenties would be nice, but paying bills and managing debt are usually the pressing issues. So it wasn't Carstensen's focus on retirement that caught my interest. What intrigued me was her method.

Carstensen used virtual reality to help twentysomethings

imagine their future selves. In one condition of her experiment, twenty-five subjects entered an immersive virtual reality environment and, in a virtual mirror, they saw digital representations of their current selves. In the other condition, twenty-five different subjects entered the same virtual reality environment, but rather than seeing their current digital selves in the mirror, they saw an age-morphed version of their future selves. The second group of twentysomethings saw a projection of what they would look like when they were old.

After the subjects emerged from the virtual environment, they were told to allocate money toward a hypothetical retirement savings account. The subjects who had seen their current selves in the mirror set aside payments averaging $73.90. Those who saw their future selves set aside more than twice that amount, payments averaging $178.10.

This study brings to life, at least digitally, a core problem in behavior: present bias. People of all ages and walks of life discount the future, favoring the rewards of today over the rewards of tomorrow. We would rather have $100 this month than $150 next month. We choose the chocolate cake and the new outfit now and face the gym and the credit card bill later. This isn't a twentysomething tendency. It's a human tendency, one that underpins addiction, procrastination, health, oil consumption, and, yes, saving for retirement. It is often difficult to imagine and give weight to things that will happen down the line.

But twentysomethings are *especially* prone to present bias. Their brains are still developing the forward thinking it takes to anticipate consequences and plan for the future. And when they do turn to close friends or older others with nervous questions about their lives, they often receive pats on the head and stock phrases like "It'll work out. You have all the time in the world."

At the same time, twentysomething exploits are met with more enthusiastic clichés, such as "You're only young once" or "Have fun while you can." These messages encourage risk-taking and what one researcher calls "now-or-never behaviors" that don't actually make us happy for long: partying, multiple sex partners, blowing off responsibilities, being lazy, not having a real job.

Again and again, twentysomethings hear they have infinite time for the dreaded adult things but so little time for the purportedly good stuff. This makes living in the present easy. It's connecting the present with the future that takes work.

I was browsing in a clothing store one afternoon when I overheard two twentysomething sales clerks talking as they folded shirts. The male clerk said to the female clerk something like this: "Everyone tells me I should stop smoking cigars. Why should I? So I can live to be ninety-five instead of eighty-five? Who wants to have ten extra years when you're old and all your friends are dead and you have no life? If quitting smoking meant I could do my twenties again, I'd do it. But I'm twenty-eight. Why should I stop having fun now just to get really old and be in my nineties?"

I kind of wanted to throw the clerk into a virtual reality chamber and show him that lung cancer is awful at any age. Or at least chat with him about how he would feel if he were still folding clothes at thirty-one. But I wasn't at work, so I bit my tongue.

For the rest of that day, and for many days, I thought about what this young man said. It wasn't about cigars or even health. It was about time. I got the point about living in the present, but what I most noticed was that, for him, it was as if there was nothing between the ages of twenty-eight and eighty-five. Life consisted of being twentysomething or nearly dead. There was no mention of what might go on in his thirties or forties or sixties or seventies, much less the idea that he might want to be around—and well—for it. He could not imagine himself as anything other than a twentysomething whose life revolved around his friends, but the rest of his life was going to come all the same.

Many cultures make use of *memento mori* to remind us of our mortality, the skeletons and dying flowers often represented in art or on display in the marketplace. In past centuries, it was common to sit for portraits while holding a dead rose or to carry a watch shaped like a skull in order to signify time running out. In my practice, I notice that many twentysomethings—especially those who surround themselves with other twentysomethings—have trouble anticipating *life.* They need *memento vivi*—or ways to remember they are going to live. They need something to remind them that life is going to continue on past their twenties, and that it might even be great.

Rachel had been tending bar at a restaurant since dropping out of a master's program in public health. She didn't like the field of health research and thought she and her American Studies major would be better suited to law. The problem was, in the two years that had passed since leaving grad school, she hadn't made a move toward getting a JD.

Rachel worked the night shift, so she often closed the place down and partied inside with the other servers. Then she slept in and spent her afternoons trying to see friends who weren't at work. After one night out, a female friend slept over at her place only to spring out of bed at ten a.m., saying, "Oh my gosh, I can't believe I slept this late! I have a million things to do. I have to go!" Rachel came to my office that day feeling uncomfortably self-aware that she regularly slept until noon. "I stay so distracted," she said. "I just can't keep track of time."

When I asked what kept her so distracted, Rachel complained her work schedule left her out of sync with the rest of the world. Then, she said, there were always errands and boy drama and days spent "watching *Law & Order* marathons and having magical thoughts." Even when Rachel was trying to get things done, she said, it was just so easy not to. "I stare at my computer and try to deal with writing an old TA to get a letter of recommendation for law school or something, and I know I should, but I feel so relieved when someone chats me or a text comes in," she said. "I get to think about something else instead."

Rachel came to her session one afternoon after subbing on the lunch shift. She slung her bag on the couch and grunted as she sat down. "I am so sick of restaurants, and I *hate* the lunch crowd. There's all these customers that come in and they treat the servers and bartenders like crap. And I keep thinking I could have their jobs if I wanted," she said.

When clients get tired of doing something, and I get tired of hearing about something, that often means it's time for a change. "Let's talk about that," I said. "You could have whose jobs?"

"The lawyers. They're no smarter than I am…"

"OK, good. They probably aren't any smarter than you are. But there are some things that set them apart right now."

"Like law school. I know."

"It's more than that. There's LSAT prep and the LSAT. Applications. Reference letters. Interviews. Three years of law school with summer internships. The bar. And then time to get going in a new job."

"I know. I *know*," she growled.

I sat for a moment, waiting for Rachel to be less irritated by me. Then I said, "It must feel like I'm pressuring you."

"I know you're just doing your job. But people do things later than they used to. People's lives really happen in their thirties now."

I thought about my thirtysomething clients and said, "There is a big difference between *having* a life in your thirties and *starting* a life in your thirties." I walked over to my desk and got out a clipboard and some paper and a pencil. "I'm making a timeline. Help me fill this in."

"*Not* a timeline," Rachel drawled with a look of dread. "I'm not going to be one of those girls with the engagement ring app on my phone while I'm still single. I tell everybody I'm getting married at forty and having my first kid at forty-five. I do *not* want a timeline."

"It sounds like you need one," I replied.

Present bias is especially strong in twentysomethings who put a lot of psychological distance between now and later. Love or work can seem far off in time, like the way that Rachel tossed marriage and kids decades into the future. The future can also seem socially distant when we hang out with people who are not talking about it either. Later can even feel spatially far away if we imagine ultimately settling down in some other place.

The problem with feeling distant from the future is that distance leads to abstraction, and abstraction leads to distance, and round and round it goes. The further away love and work seem, the less we need to think about them; the less we think about love and work, the further away they feel. I started to sketch out a timeline to bring the future closer and to make Rachel's thinking more concrete.

"You're twenty-six. When are you going to turn toward law school?" I asked with my pencil ready.

"I don't know exactly. Your timeline is making me nervous," she laughed, "so I hate to commit to next year or something. But definitely by thirty. I definitely will *not* be bartending at thirty."

"OK. If you start the law school process up at thirty, there are three years of law school. At least a year before school to take the LSAT, do your applications, and get reference letters. Probably an additional year afterward to pass the bar and start a job. That's five years minimum. So if you get going at thirty you'd be one of those lawyers in the restaurant in about five years. You'd be thirty-five. How does that sound?"

"That could be all right. . . ."

"When did you say you wanted to get married? Forty?" I wrote that in.

Rachel started to look hesitant.

"And baby at forty-five? Really?"

"No, not really. I just mean that stuff is all way far off for me. I'm not worrying about that now."

"Exactly. You're leaving it in this far-off, abstracted place. When would you actually like for marriage or kids to happen?" I asked, erasing.

"I'd definitely like to have my first child by thirty-five and marriage sometime before that, probably. I don't want to be an older, *older* mom."

"That sounds more informed," I said as I revised the timeline. "So between thirty and thirty-five, you envision law school plus marriage plus baby. That's going to be a tight five years. How do you feel about having a baby in law school?"

"That sounds kind of awful. No, I don't see that. Plus I might not want to work full-time right after I have a kid."

"Can you get married and have a baby now?"

"No! Dr. Jay! I'm not even in a relationship!"

"Rachel, your life is not adding up. You plan to do all those things between thirty and thirty-five, but you say you don't want to do them all at the same time."

"No, I don't."

"Then now is the time for school."

"I guess now is when I should also stop dating random people I don't really want to be around that much," Rachel said.

"Probably so," I answered.

Once law school seemed less distant for Rachel, it became more concrete. Rachel bought books about getting into law school. She made a list of everything standing between her and her lawyer customers at the restaurant. She quit bartending and started a job at a law firm so she could scrape together some reference letters. She put her efforts into getting an LSAT score that would offset her shaky college years.

About two years later, Rachel headed to law school in Pennsylvania.

Rachel had heard that "people do things later than they used to," but what this really meant for her twenties was unclear. Once she could envision what she wanted her thirtysomething life to look like, what to do with the twentysomething years became more urgent and more defined. A timeline may not be a virtual reality chamber, but it can help our brains see time for what it really is: limited. It can give us a reason to get up in the morning and get going.

Our twenties are when we have to start creating our own sense of time, our own plans about how the years ahead will unfold. It is difficult to know how to start our careers or when to start our families. It is tempting to stay distracted and keep everything at a distance. But twentysomethings who live beyond time usually aren't happy. It's like living in a cave where we never know what time it is or what we ought to do or why, sometimes until it is too late.

Partway through law school, Rachel sent this:

> I thought if I didn't participate in adulthood, time would stop. But it didn't. It just kept going. People around me kept going. Now I see I need to get going—and keep going. I try to plan things in the future to work toward—5K runs or my summer internship—so I keep practicing being more future-oriented.
>
> Plus, my best friend here is a med resident. She's thirty-three—five years older than me almost exactly—and we talk about twenty million times a day. It's crazy to me that she is out

> of her twenties and yet where she is and what she is doing with her life don't seem too far away from where I am. It just makes me realize that my twenties are going to fly by, so I kind of want to make sure I take the time to experience this sort of unencumbered, unattached few years that I have here. That being said, I'm glad to be in school and I'm even working in a legal clinic in town. Actually, I'm thrilled to have health insurance and a 401(k). I want to enjoy my twenties but I want the happy ending too.

How do you get the happy ending? John Irving ought to know. One of my favorite authors, Irving writes these multigenerational epics of fiction that somehow work out in the end. How does he do it? He says, "I always begin with the last sentence; then I work my way backwards, through the plot, to where the story should begin." That sounds like a lot of work, especially compared to the fantasy that great writers sit down and just go where the story takes them. Irving lets us know that good stories, and happy endings, are more intentional than that.

Most twentysomethings can't write the last sentence of their lives, but when pressed, they usually can identify things they want in their thirties or forties or sixties—or things they don't want—and work backward from there. This is how you have your own multigenerational epic with a happy ending. This is how you live your life in real time.

EPILOGUE

Will Things Work Out for Me?

The best part about being my age is knowing how my life worked out.

—Scott Adams, cartoonist

There is a sign just outside of Rocky Mountain National Park that reads in big, bold letters: MOUNTAINS DON'T CARE. It is a sign about preparedness, and it goes on to educate mountain-goers about lightning, avalanches, and proper equipment. I was about twenty-five years old when I first saw this sign. It was scary, but I remember liking it immediately. It meant something to me that the sign was telling it like it is. It was reminding me that, when I went into the wilderness, I had to know what I was getting into and I had to be ready. If I got caught on a peak in a late-afternoon lightning storm, it wasn't going to matter whether I meant to get off the mountain sooner or even whether I was a really nice person. Adulthood is sort of like that. There are things that just are what they are. The smartest thing to do is know as much about them as you can.

In one way or another, almost every twentysomething client I have wonders, "Will things work out for me?" The uncertainty behind that question is what makes twentysomething life so difficult, but it is also what makes twentysomething action so possible and so necessary. It's unsettling to not know the future and, in a way, even more daunting to consider that what we are doing with our twentysomething lives might be determining it. It is almost a relief to imagine that these years aren't real, that twentysomething jobs and relationships don't count. But a career spent studying adult development tells me this is far from true. And years of listening closely to clients and students tells me that, deep down, twentysomethings want to be taken seriously, and they want their lives to be taken seriously. They want to know that what they do matters—and it does.

There is no formula for a good life, and there is no right or wrong life. But there are choices and consequences, so it seems only fair that twentysomethings know about the ones that lie ahead. That way, the future feels good when you finally get there. The nicest part about getting older is knowing how your life worked out, especially if you like what you wake up to every day. If you are paying attention to your life as a twentysomething, the real glory days are still to come.

I saw the MOUNTAINS DON'T CARE sign when I was headed into the Rockies on a backpacking trip. Probably because the sign unnerved me, I stopped in at the backcountry office to clear my itinerary with the ranger. To get to the first valley where I would camp, I needed to walk some miles in and hike switchback up the scree of a mountain. Then I would cut diagonally across a steep snow slope to get to t[illegible] between two peaks. There I could pop over the ridg[illegible] down the other side before nightfall.

This wasn't especially dangerous, given that I was experienced and had the right gear. But I did need to get to the snow slope fast enough so I could cross it before too many hours of heat from the sun made it susceptible to slide. I knew the pace at which I needed to hike and the angle of the slope, but still I felt nervous.

As I gathered up my maps and turned to go, I hesitated and asked the ranger, "Am I going to make it?"

He looked at me and said, "You haven't decided yet."

At the time, I thought this man was not a particularly good backcountry ranger. Now I have to laugh. He was telling me what I say to my twentysomething clients every day, what this book has been all about. The future isn't written in the stars. There are no guarantees. So claim your adulthood. Be intentional. Get to work. Pick your family. Do the math. Make your own certainty. Don't be defined by what you didn't know or didn't do.

You are deciding your life right now.

NOTES

PREFACE
THE DEFINING DECADE

[p. xi] ***Researchers at Boston University and University of Michigan***: See W. R. Mackavey, J. E. Malley, and A. J. Stewart's article "Remembering Autobiographically Consequential Experiences: Content Analysis of Psychologists' Accounts of Their Lives" in *Psychology and Aging* 6 (1991): 50–59. In this study, autobiographically consequential events were divided by developmental stage, not by ten-year period. To determine which decade of life contained the most consequential experiences, I reanalyzed the data by finding the average number of consequential events per year in each developmental period. Then I weighted each year individually with those average scores, making cut points at the decades rather than at developmental periods.

INTRODUCTION
REAL TIME

[p. xvii] ***When Kate's parents were in their twenties***: For a comprehensive account of how the baby boomer generation differs from twenty-first-century twentysomethings, see Neil Howe and William Strauss's book *Millennials Rising: The Next Great Generation* (New York: Vintage, 2000).

[p. xvii] ***The median home price in the United States was $17,000***: Historic home values can be found online at http://www.census.gov/hhes/www/housing/census/historic/values.html.

[p. xvii] ***An enormous cultural shift***: For up-to-date information on twenty-first-century twentysomethings, see the Pew Research Center 2010 report "Millennials: Confident. Connected. Open to Change," found at http://pewresearch.org/millennials.

[p. xviii] ***"Bridget Jones Economy"***: See "The Bridget Jones Economy: Singles and the City—How Young Singles Shape City Culture, Lifestyles, and Economics" in *The Economist*, December 22, 2001.

[p. xviii] ***"Meet the Twixters"***: From the Sunday, January 16, 2005, cover article for *Time* magazine, titled "Meet the Twixters," by Lev Grossman. Grossman provides a comprehensive, popular article about the economic, sociological, and cultural changes that have contributed to twentysomethings' feeling of being betwixt and between.

[p. xviii] ***The Odyssey Years***: From "The Odyssey Years" by David Brooks for the *New York Times*, dated October 9, 2007.

[p. xviii] ***Emerging adulthood***: Researcher Jeffrey Jensen Arnett coined the term "emerging adulthood" to refer to those aged eighteen to twenty-five. Arnett has done much excellent research on this age group, some of which is included in this book. I draw on Arnett's research but not on the term "emerging adult" because I am discussing all of the twentysomething years. Also, I don't think you empower twentysomethings by essentially telling them they are not adults.

Notes

[p. xviii] ***"Not-quite-adults"***: See Richard Settersten and Barbara E. Ray's book *Not Quite Adults: Why 20-Somethings Are Choosing a Slower Path to Adulthood, and Why It's Good for Everyone* (New York: Bantam Books, 2010).

[p. xix] ***Amortality***: See "10 Ideas Changing the World Right Now" by Catherine Mayer for *Time* magazine, March 12, 2009.

[p. xix] ***Difficult for twentysomethings to gain a foothold at home***: For a thorough examination of the postmodern economy and its consequences, read Richard Sennett's article "The New Political Economy and Its Culture" in *The Hedgehog Review* 12 (2000): 55–71.

[p. xx] ***Unemployment is at its highest in decades***: Find current statistics at the Bureau of Labor Statistics, http://www.bls.gov/cps.

[p. xx] ***An unpaid internship is the new starter job***: For an article about the competition for unpaid internships, read "Unpaid Work, But They Pay for Privilege" by Gerry Shih for the *New York Times*, August 8, 2009.

[p. xx] ***About a quarter of twentysomethings are out of work***: For up-to-date information on twenty-first-century twentysomethings, see the Pew Research Center 2010 report "Millennials: Confident. Connected. Open to Change," found at http://pewresearch.org/millennials.

[p. xx] ***Twentysomethings . . . earn less than their 1970s counterparts***: In addition to Pew, for another source of up-to-date information on young adulthood in the United States, see the Network on Transitions to Adulthood at www.transitions2adulthood.com.

[p. xx]: ***One-third will move in any given year***: See chapter 1 of Jeffrey Jensen Arnett's book *Emerging Adulthood: The Winding Road from the Late Teens through the Twenties* (New York: Oxford University Press, 2004).

Notes

[p. xx] ***The number of students owing more than $40,000***: See the Project on Student Debt at http://projectonstudentdebt.org.

[p. xxii] ***"The kids are actually sort of alright"***: See "The Kids Are Actually Sort of Alright" by Noreen Malone for *New York* magazine, October 24, 2011.

[p. xxii] ***"Hope is a good breakfast but a bad supper"***: This quote comes from Sir Francis Bacon.

[p. xxiii] ***Harder to do all at the same time in our thirties***: See S. M. Bianchi's paper "Family Change and Time Allocation in American Families," presented at the November 2010 conference for Focus on Workplace Flexibility. The paper can be found at http://workplaceflexibility.org. Bianchi's research is discussed further in the chapter "Every Body."

[p. xxiv] ***There is what is called a critical period***: "Sensitive period" is the correct technical term. A *critical* period is actually a time during which, if something does not develop, it simply cannot develop later. A *sensitive* period is a time during which it is easiest for something to develop. I use the term "critical period" because it is a more familiar term and it is in line with the Chomsky quote—one where he also blurs the difference between a sensitive period and critical period—at the beginning of the chapter.

[p. xxv] ***"What Is It About Twentysomethings?"***: See "What Is It About 20-Somethings?" by Robin Marantz Henig for the *New York Times,* August 18, 2010.

[p. xxv] ***"Why Won't They Just Grow Up?"***: Taken from the Sunday, January 16, 2005, cover article for *Time* magazine, titled "Meet the Twixters," by Lev Grossman.

Notes

Identity Capital

[p. 5] ***"Have you ever heard of Erik Erikson?"***: Erikson's story has been written about in many places. For a comprehensive account, see Lawrence J. Friedman's book *Identity's Architect: A Biography of Erik Erikson* (New York: Scribner, 1999).

[p. 6] ***Identity capital***: A term introduced by sociologist James Côté. For a fuller explanation, see pages 208–212 in Côté's book *Arrested Adulthood: The Changing Nature of Maturity and Identity* (New York: New York University Press, 2000).

[p. 7] ***"Disengaged confusion"***: From Erik Erikson's classic book *Identity: Youth and Crisis* (New York: Norton, 1968).

[p. 7] ***Construct stronger identities***: See J. E. Marcia's research paper "Development and Validation of Ego-Identity Status" in *Journal of Personality and Social Psychology* 3 (1966): 551–558; J. E. Côté and S. J. Schwartz's article "Comparing Psychological and Social Approaches to Identity: Identity Status, Identity Capital, and the Individualization Process" in *Journal of Adolescence* 25 (2002): 571–586; and S. J. Schwartz, J. E. Côté, and J. J. Arnett's article "Identity and Agency in Emerging Adulthood: Two Developmental Routes in the Individuation Process" in *Youth Society* 2 (2005): 201–220.

[p. 12] ***"Different and damaged"***: This quote comes from "How a New Jobless Era Will Transform America" by Don Peck for *The Atlantic,* March 2010.

[p. 12] ***Less motivated than their peers***: In "Stop-Gap Jobs Rob Graduates of Ambition," Rosemary Bennett reports on new research by Tony Cassidy and Liz Wright presented to the British Psychological Society in *The Times* (London), April 5, 2008.

[p. 12] ***Twentysomething unemployment is associated with heavy drinking and depression***: See K. Mossakowski's research article "Is the Duration of Poverty and Unemployment a Risk Factor for Heavy Drinking?" in *Social Science and Medicine* 67 (2008): pages 947–955.

[p. 12] ***Twentysomething work has an inordinate influence***: See "How a New Jobless Era Will Transform America" by Don Peck for *The Atlantic,* March 2010, as well as "Hello, Young Workers: The Best Way to Reach the Top Is to Start There" by Austan Goolsbee for the *New York Times,* May 25, 2006.

[p. 12] ***Salaries peak—and plateau—in our forties***: See "The Other Midlife Crisis" by Ellen E. Schultz and Jessica Silver-Greenberg for the *Wall Street Journal,* June 18, 2011.

Weak Ties

[p. 19] ***Urban Tribe***: There is some dispute about who coined this term, Michel Maffesoli, a French sociologist who wrote *Le temps des tribus: Le déclin de l'individualisme dans les sociétés de masses* (*The Time of Tribes: The Decline of Individualism in Postmodern Society*) in 1988, or Ethan Watters, an American author who wrote about urban tribes in a *New York Times Magazine* article in 2001 and then in a book titled *Urban Tribes* in 2003.

[p. 20] ***"The Strength of Weak Ties"***: M. Granovetter's defining works on the subject are an article "The Strength of Weak Ties" in *American Journal of Sociology* 78 (1973): 1360–1380 and his 1983 follow-up paper, "The Strength of Weak Ties: A Network Theory Revisited" in *Sociological Theory* 1 (1983): 201–233.

Notes

[p. 21] ***"Similarity breeds connection"***: In M. McPherson, L. Smith-Lovin, and J. M. Cook's article "Birds of a Feather: Homophily in Social Networks" in *Annual Review of Sociology* 27 (2001): 415–444. The quote is on page 415.

[p. 21]: ***A homogeneous clique***: See D. M. Boyd and N. B. Ellison's article "Social Network Sites: Definition, History, and Scholarship" in *Journal of Computer-Mediated Communication* 13 (2008): 210–230.

[p. 21] ***"Weakness of strong ties"***: See R. Coser's article "The Complexity of Roles as a Seedbed of Individual Autonomy" in *The Idea of Social Structure: Papers in Honor of Robert K. Merton,* edited by L. A. Coser (New York: Harcourt Brace Jovanovich, 1975); the quote can be found on page 242. See also Rose Coser's book *In Defense of Modernity* (Stanford, CA: Stanford University Press, 1991), for how complex and multiple social roles nurture richer individuals.

[p. 22] ***Restricted speech***: See B. Bernstein's article "Elaborated and Restricted Codes: Their Social Origins and Some Consequences" in *American Anthropologist* 66 (1964): 55–69.

[p. 28] ***I did not . . . aim at gaining his favour***: This quote can be found on pages 216–217 of *The Autobiography of Benjamin Franklin,* edited by J. Bigelow (Philadelphia: Lippincott, 1900, facsimile of the 1868 original).

[p. 28] ***Ben Franklin effect, and subsequent empirical studies***: For a discussion of what later came to be called the Ben Franklin effect, see J. Jecker and D. Landy's article "Liking a Person as a Function of Doing Him a Favour" in *Human Relations* 22 (1968): 371–378. For the classic article outlining the foot-in-the-door technique, see J. L. Freedman and S. C. Fraser's article "Compliance without Pressure: The

Foot-in-the-Door Technique" in *Journal of Personality and Social Psychology* 4 (1966): 195–202.

[p. 29] ***It's good to be good***: See S. G. Post's article "Altruism, Happiness, and Health: It's Good to Be Good" in *International Journal of Behavioral Medicine* 12 (2005): 66–77.

[p. 29] ***"Helper's high"***: See A. Luks's article "Doing Good: Helper's High" in *Psychology Today* 22 (1988): 39–40.

[p. 29] ***Part of aging well is helping others***: Erik Erikson not only wrote about young adulthood, he was also the first psychologist to propose a psychosocial stage model of development that spanned from birth to death. The last two stages of Erikson's eight-stage model are Generativity and Ego Integrity. These stages take place in middle and later adulthood, and both include striving toward feeling purposeful and accomplished. Helping others is one way that adults add meaning to their lives.

[p. 31] ***Research shows that our social networks* narrow *across adulthood***: See L. L. Carstensen, D. M. Isaacowitz, and S. T. Charles's article "Taking Time Seriously: A Theory of Socioemotional Selectivity" in *American Psychologist* 54 (1999): 165–181.

The Unthought Known

[p. 35] ***The jam experiment***: See S. Iyengar and M. Lepper's article "When Choice Is Demotivating: Can One Desire Too Much of a Good Thing?" in *Journal of Personality and Social Psychology* 79 (2000): 995–1006, as well as Iyengar's book *The Art of Choosing* (New York: Twelve, 2010).

[p. 39] ***The unthought known***: A phrase coined by psychoanalyst Christopher Bollas.

Notes

My Life Should Look Better on Facebook

[p. 43] ***Some 90 percent of users say they use Facebook***: See J. B. Walther, B. Van Der Heide, S-Y Kim, D. Westerman, and S. T. Tong's article "The Role of Friends' Appearance and Behavior on Evaluations of Individuals on Facebook: Are We Known by the Company We Keep?" in *Human Communication Research* 34 (2008): 28–49.

[p. 44] ***Facebook users spend more time***: See T. A. Pempek, Y. A. Yermolayeva, and S. L. Calvert's article "College Students' Social Networking Experiences on Facebook" in *Journal of Applied Developmental Psychology* 30 (2009): 227–238.

[p. 44] ***In one study, nearly four hundred participants***: See J. B. Walther, B. Van Der Heide, S-Y Kim, D. Westerman, and S. T. Tong's article "The Role of Friends' Appearance and Behavior on Evaluations of Individuals on Facebook: Are We Known by the Company We Keep?" in *Human Communication Research* 34 (2008): 28–49.

[p. 45] ***Way of keeping up***: A. Joinson's study "Looking At, Looking Up, or Keeping Up with People? Motives and Uses of Facebook," presented at the Proceeding of the 26th Annual SIGCHI Conference on Human Factors in Computing Systems (2008). Also see C. Lampe, N. Ellison, and C. Steinfield's article "A Face(book) in the Crowd: Social Searching vs. Social Browsing," presented at the Proceedings of the 2006 20th Anniversary Conference on Computer Supported Cooperative Work.

[p. 47] ***Half of recent graduates working in jobs***: See "Many with New College Degree Find the Job Market Humbling" by Catherine Rampell for the *New York Times,* May 18, 2011.

[p. 49] ***Search for glory*** and ***tyranny of the should***: Karen Horney coined the phrases "tyranny of the shoulds" and the "search for glory." These distortions of development are described in her book *Neurosis and Human Growth.* The 40th Anniversary Edition was published in 1991 (New York: Norton).

The Customized Life

[p. 54] ***Customized life***: I use the term "customized life" in this chapter because I was drawing from my client Ian's own experience. But the idea that readymade lives are no longer available and that the burden is on youth to put together the pieces of a self and a life is one that has been advanced by other theorists. Those I have drawn on most heavily in my work with twentysomethings are psychologist Erik Erikson and sociologists James Côté and Richard Sennett.

[p. 56] ***"The dread of doing what has been done before"***: This quote is from Edith Wharton.

[p. 56] ***Distinctiveness is a fundamental part of identity***: See V. L. Vignoles, X. Chryssochoou, and G. M. Breakwell's article "The Distinctiveness Principle: Identity, Meaning, and the Bounds of Cultural Relativity" in *Personality and Social Psychology Review* 4 (2000): 337–354.

[p. 59] ***Mass customization***: Stan Davis coined the term "mass customization" in his book *Future Perfect* (New York: Basic Books, 1987).

[p. 60] ***Companies and marketers have tapped into the innovative life***: For an introduction into how product customization allows consumers to express uniqueness and achieve better fit, see N. Franke and M. Schreier's article "Why Customers Value Mass-

Customized Projects: The Importance of Process Effort and Enjoyment" in *Journal of Product Innovation Management* 27 (2010): 1020–1031, and N. Franke and M. Schreier's article "Product Uniqueness as a Driver of Customer Utility in Mass Customization" in *Marketing Letters* 19 (2007): 93–107.

[p. 60] ***"Let them eat lifestyle!"***: From Thomas Frank's *Conglomerates and the Media* (New York: The New Press, 1997), excerpt available online from *Utne Reader* at http://www.utne.com/1997-11-01/let-them-eat-lifestyle.aspx. Also see Frank's *The Conquest of Cool: Business Culture, Counterculture, and the Rise of Hip Consumerism* (Chicago: University of Chicago Press, 1998).

An Upmarket Conversation

[p. 69] ***In 2009, David Brooks wrote an article***: See "Advice for High School Graduates" by David Brooks for the *New York Times,* June 10, 2009.

[p. 70] ***Hooking up is the new relational medium***: See "The Demise of Dating" by Charles M. Blow for the *New York Times,* December 13, 2008.

[p. 70] ***Young Americans do marry later***: From Vital and Health Statistics report from the CDC: "Cohabitation, Marriage, Divorce, and Remarriage in the United States" released in July 2002, available online at http://www.cdc.gov/nchs/data/series/sr_23/sr23_022.pdf.

[p. 70] ***The average age for first marriage is twenty-six***: See 2009 table from United States Census Bureau, "Median Age at First Marriage, by Sex: 1890 to the Present" at www.census.gov.

[p. 71] ***Obsessed with avoiding commitment***: See Kay Hymowitz's 2008 articles for *City Journal* "Child-Man in the Promised Land: Today's Single Young

Men Hang Out in a Hormonal Libido Between Adolescence and Adulthood" and "Love in the Time of Darwinism: A Report from the Chaotic Postfeminist Dating Scene, Where Only the Strong Survive," both available online at www.city-journal.org.

[p. 71] ***Educational consultants charge as much as $30,000***: See "In College Entrance Frenzy, a Lesson Out of Left Field" by Samuel F. Freedman for the *New York Times,* April 26, 2006.

[p. 71] ***Internship-placement services can cost thousands***: See "Unpaid Work, but They Pay for Privilege" by Gerry Shih for the *New York Times,* August 8, 2009.

[p. 72] ***"Remarriage is the triumph of hope over experience"***: This quote is from Samuel Johnson, and also appears on page 114 in J. J. Arnett's *Emerging Adulthood: The Winding Road from the Late Teens Through the Twenties* (New York: Oxford University Press, 2004).

[p. 73] ***"The unexpected legacy of divorce"***: A must-read for any child of divorce, or any divorced parent, is *The Unexpected Legacy of Divorce: A 25-Year Landmark Study* by Judith S. Wallerstein, Julia M. Lewis, and Sandra Blakeslee (New York: Hyperion, 2000).

[p. 73] ***The divorce rate holds steady at about 40 percent***: From Vital and Health Statistics report from the CDC: "Cohabitation, Marriage, Divorce, and Remarriage in the United States" released in July 2002, available online at http://www.cdc.gov/nchs/data/series/sr_23/sr23_022.pdf.

[p. 73] ***A study that followed about a hundred women***: The Mills Longitudinal Study is a fifty-year study of adult development that has followed about one hundred women who graduated from Mills College in Oakland, California, in the early 1960s. One of the longest running studies of women in the world, the

Mills Study has generated more than one hundred scholarly publications. The study is currently housed at the University of California, Berkeley, and is run by principal investigators Ravenna Helson and Oliver P. John.

[p. 74] ***The later the better***: For a review of the theoretical perspectives on the relationship between age of marriage and marital success, as well as preliminary data that show that later marriages may be less happy, see N. D. Glenn, J. E. Uecker, and R.W.B. Love Jr.'s article "Later First Marriage and Marital Success" in *Social Science Research* 39 (2010): 787–800.

[p. 74] ***The Age Thirty Deadline***: This term is coined in J. J. Arnett's book *Emerging Adulthood: The Winding Road from the Late Teens Through the Twenties* (New York: Oxford University Press, 2004).

Picking Your Family

[p. 82] ***Parlay being talkative into social status***: For an interesting study of how extraversion leads to higher status in groups, see C. Anderson, O. P. John, D. Keltner, and A. M. Kring's article "Who Attains Social Status? Effects of Personality and Physical Attractiveness in Social Groups" in *Journal of Personality and Social Psychology* 81 (2001): 116–132.

[p. 82] ***Intelligence aids achievement***: See Arthur Jensen's *Bias in Mental Testing* (New York: Free Press, 1980).

[p. 82] ***Successful people are generally brimming with confidence***: For an overview of self-efficacy and how it translates into success, see the definitive work by Albert Bandura, *Self-Efficacy: The Exercise of Control* (New York: Worth Publishers, 1997).

[p. 86] ***"Weekend with Boyfriend's Parents Explains a Lot"***: I found the article Emma was referring to, and it is indeed funny. See "Weekend with Boyfriend's Parents Explains a Lot" in *The Onion,* Issue 38-02, dated January 23, 2002.

The Cohabitation Effect

[p. 91] ***Cohabitation in the United States has increased***: See D. Popenoe's "Cohabitation, Marriage, and Child Well-Being" available from the National Marriage Project at http://www.virginia.edu/marriageproject.

[p. 91] ***"You would only marry someone if he or she agreed to live together with you first"***: For this statistic, see D. Popenoe and B. D. Whitehead's 2001 "State of Our Unions" available from the National Marriage Project at http://www.virginia.edu/marriageproject.

[p. 91] ***The cohabitation effect***: For scholarly research on the cohabitation effect, see C. C. Cohan and S. Kleinbaum's article "Toward a Greater Understanding of the Cohabitation Effect: Premarital Cohabitation and Marital Communication" in *Journal of Marriage and Family* 64 (2004):180–192, and S. M. Stanley, G. K. Rhoades, and H. J. Markman's article "Sliding Versus Deciding: Inertia and the Premarital Cohabitation Effect" in *Family Relations* 55 (2006): 499–509.

[p. 92] ***Cohabitation effect is not fully explained by individual characteristics***: See the 2008 "State of Our Unions" from the National Marriage Project at http://www.virginia.edu/marriageproject.

[p. 92] ***It "just happened"***: See J. M. Lindsay's article "An Ambiguous Commitment: Moving into a Cohabitation Relationship" in *Journal of Family Studies* 6 (2000): 120–134; S. M. Stanley, G. K. Rhoades, and H. J. Markman, "Sliding Versus Deciding"; and W. D. Manning and P. J. Smock's article "Measuring and Modeling Cohabitation: New Perspectives from Qualitative Data" in *Journal of Marriage and Family* 67 (2005): 989–1002.

[p. 92] ***"Sliding, not deciding"***: See S. M. Stanley, G. K. Rhoades, and H. J. Markman's article "Sliding Versus Deciding: Inertia and the Premarital Cohabitation Effect" in *Family Relations* 55 (2006): 499–509.

[p. 94] ***Couples who live together* before an engagement**: See "Cohabitation, Marriage, Divorce, and Remarriage in the United States" from the Centers for Disease Control and Prevention, Vital and Health Statistics, Series 23, Number 22, July 2002, as well as "Marriage and Cohabitation in the United States" also from the Centers for Disease Control and Prevention, Vital and Health Statistics, Series 23, Number 28, February 2010.

[p. 95] ***Less dedicated before, and even after, marriage***: See G. K. Rhoades, S. M. Scott, and H. J. Markman's article "The Pre-Engagement Cohabitation Effect: A Replication and Extension of Previous Findings" in *Journal of Family Psychology* 23 (2009): 107–111; G. H. Kline, S. M. Scott, H. J. Markman, P. A. Olmos-Gallo, M. St. Peters, S. W. Whitton, and L. M. Prado's article "Timing Is Everything: Pre-Engagement Cohabitation and Increased Risk for Poor Marital Outcomes" in *Journal of Family Psychology* 18 (2004): 311–318; and G. K. Rhoades, S. M. Scott, and H. J. Markman's article "Pre-Engagement Cohabitation and Gender Asymmetry in Marital Commitment" in *Journal of Family Psychology* 20 (2006): 553–560.

[p. 96] ***Lock-in***: See any research on lock-in and intertemporal discounting, especially G. Zauberman's paper "The Intertemporal Dynamics of Consumer Lock-in" in *Journal of Consumer Research* 30 (2003): 405–419.

[p. 99] ***Researchers also recommend getting clear on . . . commitment level***: See S. M. Stanley, G. K. Rhoades, and H. J. Markman, "Sliding Versus Deciding."

On Dating Down

[p. 103] ***Patient's attempt at self-cure***: This insight comes from Masud Khan's paper "Toward an Epistemology of Cure" published in his book *The Privacy of the Self* (New York: International Universities Press, 1974).

[p. 108] ***The time when we have our most self-defining memories***: See D. C. Rubin, T. A. Rahhal, and L. W. Poon's study "Things Learned in Early Adulthood Are Remembered Best" in *Memory & Cognition* 26 (1998): 3–19, as well as A. Thorne's article "Personal Memory Telling and Personality Development" in *Personality and Social Psychology Review* 4 (2000): 45–56.

[p. 108] ***Adolescence is . . . our first attempt to form life stories***: See T. Habermas and S. Bluck's paper "Getting a Life: The Emergence of the Life Story in Adolescence" in *Psychological Bulletin* 126 (2000): 748–769, as well as M. Pasupathi's paper "The Social Construction of the Personal Past and Its Implications for Adult Development" in *Psychological Bulletin* 127 (2001): 651–672.

[p. 108] ***Stories we tell about ourselves become facets of our identity***: For work on the narrative as an aspect of identity, see the work of D. P. McAdams and J. L. Pals, especially their paper "A New Big Five: Fundamental Principles for an Integrative Science of Personality" in *American Psychologist* 61 (2006): 204–217.

[p. 108] ***Untold [stories] are no less meaningful or powerful***: See A. Thorne, K. C. McLean, and A. M. Lawrence's paper "When Remembering Is Not Enough: Reflecting on Self-Defining Memories in Late Adolescence" in *Journal of Personality* 72 (2004): 513–541.

[p. 108] ***Untold stories are most often about shame***: See B. Rimé, B. Mesquita, P. Philippot, and S. Boca's study "Beyond the Emotional Event: Six Studies on the Social Sharing of Emotion" in *Cognition & Emotion* 5 (1991): 435–465.

[p. 109] ***Bits of identity with perhaps the greatest potential for change***: See D. P. McAdams and J. L. Pals, "A New Big Five: Fundamental Principles for an Integrative Science of Personality" in *American Psychologist* 61 (2006) 204–217.

[p. 110] ***"How do you see me?"***: To understand the role of being "seen" by one's parents, and of hearing your life recounted in stories as you grow, read R. Fivush, C. A. Haden, and E. Reese's article "Elaborating on Elaborations: Role of Maternal Reminiscing Style in Cognitive and Socioemotional Development" in *Child Development* 77 (2006): 1568–1588.

Being in Like

[p. 115] ***The more similar two people are***: See C. Anderson, D. Keltner, and O. P. John's article "Emotional Convergence Between People over Time" in *Journal of Personality and Social Psychology* 84 (2003): 1054–1068; G. Gonzaga, B. Campos, and T. Bradbury's article "Similarity, Convergence, and Relationship Satisfaction in Dating and Married Couples" in *Journal of Per-*

sonality and Social Psychology 93 (2007): 34–48; S. Luo and E. C. Klohnen's paper "Assortative Mating and Marital Quality in Newlyweds: A Couple-Centered Approach" in *Journal of Personality and Social Psychology* 88 (2005): 304–326; and D. Watson, E. C. Klohnen, A. Casillas, E. Nus Simms, J. Haig, and D. S. Berry's article "Match Makers and Deal Breakers: Analyses of Assortative Mating in Newlywed Couples" in *Journal of Personality* 72 (2004): 1029–1068.

[p. 116] ***Less likely to seek divorce***: For articles about various types of couple similarities, see: E. Berscheid, K. Dion, E. Hatfield, and G. W. Walster's paper "Physical Attractiveness and Dating Choice: A Test of the Matching Hypothesis" in *Journal of Experimental Social Psychology* 7 (1971): 173–189; T. Bouchard Jr. and M. McGue's paper "Familial Studies of Intelligence: A Review" in *Science* 212 (1981): 1055–1059; D. M. Buss's paper "Human Mate Selection" in *American Scientist* 73 (1985): 47–51; A. Feingold's paper "Matching for Attractiveness in Romantic Partners and Same-Sex Friends: A Meta-Analysis and Theoretical Critique" in *Psychological Bulletin* 104 (1988): 226–235; D.T.Y. Tan and R. Singh's paper "Attitudes and Attraction: A Developmental Study of the Similarity-Attraction and Dissimilarity-Repulsion Hypotheses" in *Personality and Social Psychology Bulletin* 21 (1995): 975–986; S. G. Vandenberg's paper "Assortative Mating, or Who Marries Whom?" in *Behavior Genetics* 11 (1972): 1–21; and G. L. White's paper "Physical Attractiveness and Courtship Process" in *Journal of Personality and Social Psychology* 39 (1980): 660–668.

[p. 116] ***One match maker to consider is personality***: For papers suggesting that personality similarity increases couples' satisfaction, see G. Gonzaga, B. Campos, and T. Bradbury, "Similarity, Convergence, and Relationship Satisfaction in Dating and Married Couples"; S. Luo and E. C. Klohnen, "Assortative Mating and Marital Quality in Newlyweds"; R. Gaunt's paper "Couple Similarity and Marital Satisfaction: Are Similar Spouses Happier?" in *Journal of Personality* 74 (2006): 1401–1420; J. S. Blum and A. Mehrabian's paper "Personality and Temperament Correlates of Marital Satisfaction" in *Journal of Personality* 67 (1999): 93–125; A. Caspi and E. S. Herbener's paper "Continuity and Change: Assortative Marriage and the Consistency of Personality in Adulthood" in *Journal of Personality and Social Psychology* 58 (1990): 250–258; and R. W. Robins, A. Caspi, and T. E. Moffitt's paper "Two Personalities, One Relationship: Both Partners' Personality Traits Shape the Quality of their Relationship" in *Journal of Personality and Social Psychology* 79 (2000): 251–259. For work that suggests that personality similarity does not predict satisfaction, see K. S. Gattis, S. Berns, L. E. Simpson, and A. Christensen's article "Birds of a Feather or Strange Birds? Ties among Personality Dimensions, Similarity, and Marital Quality in *Journal of Family Psychology* 18 (2004): 564–574; and D. Watson, E. C. Klohnen, A. Casillas, E. Nus Simms, J. Haig, and D. S. Berry, "Match Makers and Deal Breakers."

[p. 116] ***Personality is how . . . couples tend to be least alike***: See H. J. Eysenck's paper "Genetic and Environmental Contributions to Individual Differences" in *Journal of Personality* 58 (1990): 245–261, as well as S. Luo and E. C. Klohnen, "Assortative Mating and Marital Quality in Newlyweds."

[p. 118] ***Couples . . . matched . . . tend to be happier***: See eHarmony Press Release "New Research Finds eHarmony Couples Are Significantly Happier in Their Marriages Than Non-eHarmony Couples" from February 2, 2006: http://www.eharmony.com/press/release/1.

[p. 118] ***Pairing people based on their personality profiles***: See S. Luo and E. C. Klohnen, "Assortative Mating and Marital Quality in Newlyweds."

[p. 118] ***Success of online dating sites is... variable***: See "Blinded by Science in the Online Dating Game" by Alina Tugend for the *New York Times,* July 17, 2009.

[p. 118] ***The Big Five***: There are numerous scholarly articles about the Big Five. For one recent and definitive article, see O. P. John, L. P. Naumann, and C. J. Soto's paper "Paradigm Shift to the Integrative Big-Five Trait Taxonomy: History, Measurement, and Conceptual Issues" in O. P. John, R. W. Robins, and L. A. Pervin (Eds.), *Handbook of Personality: Theory and Research,* Third Edition (New York: Guilford Press, 2010), pages 114–158. To measure your own Big Five, visit the following website: http://www.outofservice.com/bigfive.

[p. 118] ***The Big Five is about 50 percent inherited***: See K. L. Jang, W. J. Livesley, and P. A. Vernon's paper "Heritability and the Big Five Personality Dimensions and Their Facets: A Twin Study" in *Journal of Personality* 64 (1996): 577–591. Heritability is a population statistic. It estimates the extent to which personality is inherited in the population as a whole. A heritability estimate of 50 percent does not mean that every person's personality is exactly 50 percent inherited. Individual differences are almost always present in personality research. But a heritability estimate is a statistic that gives us a general sense of the extent to which we can expect personality to be influenced by nature (i.e., genes) versus nurture (i.e., the environment).

[p. 121] ***Evidence for personality convergence over time is mixed***: See M. N. Humbad, M. B. Donnellan, W. G. Iacono, M. McGue, and S. A. Burt's paper "Is Spousal Similarity for Personality a Matter of Convergence or Selection?" in *Personality and Individual Differences* 49 (2010): 827–830; C. Anderson, D. Keltner, and O. P. John, "Emotional Convergence Between People over Time"; and D. Watson, E. C. Klohnen, A. Casillas, E. Nus Simms, J. Haig, and D. S. Berry, "Match Makers and Deal Breakers."

[p. 121] ***"The gateway to hard work"***: Daniel Gilbert talks about how our interpersonal relationships make us more and less happy in the PBS series *This Emotional Life*. The "gateway to hard work" quote is from an NPR interview about this series. The interview can be found online at http://www.npr.org/templates/story/story.php?storyId=122207615.

[p. 124] ***Neuroticism . . . is . . . more predictive of relationship unhappiness***: For scholarly articles about negative emotionality and relationship satisfaction, see B. R. Karney and T. N. Bradbury's paper "Neuroticism, Marital Interaction and the Trajectory of Marital Satisfaction" in *Journal of Personality and Social Psychology* 72 (1997): 1075–1092; J. P. Caughlin, T. L. Huston, and R. M. Houts's paper "How Does Personality Matter in Marriage: An Examination of Trait Anxiety, Interpersonal Negativity, and Marital Satisfaction" in *Journal of Personality and Social Psychology* 78 (2000): 326–336; P. S. Dyrenforth, D. A. Kashy, M. B. Donnellan, and R. E. Lucas's paper "Predicting Relationship and Life Satisfaction from Personality in Nationally Representative Samples from Three Countries: The Relative Importance of Actor, Partner, and Similarity Effects" in *Journal of Personality and Social Psychology* 99 (2010): 690–702; and J. M. Malouff, E. B. Thorsteinsson, N. S. Schutte, N. Bhullar, and S. E. Rooke's paper "The Five-Factor Model of Personality and Relationship Satisfaction of Intimate Partners: A Meta-Analysis" in *Journal of Research in Personality* 44 (2009): 124–127.

[p. 124] ***Criticism and contempt, two leading relationship killers***: See marital expert John M. Gottman's book *What Predicts Divorce? The Relationship Between Marital Processes and Marital Outcomes* (Hillsdale, NJ: Erlbaum, 1994).

[p. 126] ***What we need in marriage changes over time***: See M. N. Shiota and R. W. Levenson's article "Birds of a Feather Don't Always Fly Farthest: Similarity in Big Five Personality Predicts More Negative Marital Satisfaction Trajectories in Long-Term Marriages" in *Personality and Aging* 22 (2007): 666–675.

Forward Thinking

[p. 133] ***Phineas Gage was a twenty-five-year-old railway worker***: For a complete historical account of Phineas Gage and his notoriety, see Malcolm Macmillan's *An Odd Kind of Fame: Stories of Phineas Gage* (Cambridge, MA: MIT Press, 2000). For the most recent findings related to Phineas Gage, see Macmillan's article "Phineas Gage—Unravelling the Myth" in the British journal *The Psychologist* 21 (2008): 828–831.

[p. 134] ***Not all was well with Phineas Gage***: This information comes from the notes of Dr. John Martyn Harlow, the physician who treated Phineas Gage immediately after his accident and then followed him for some time afterward. Harlow published three papers on Gage, in 1848, 1849, and 1868, and his notes have been reproduced in Macmillan's *An Odd Kind of Fame.*

[p. 136] ***Twentieth- and twenty-first-century patients with frontal lobe damage***: See the work of Antonio Damasio and the somatic marker hypothesis, especially the paper by A. Bechara and A. R. Damasio "The Somatic Marker Hypothesis: A Neural Theory of Economic Decision" in *Games and Economic Behavior* 52 (2004): 336–372.

[p. 137] ***The frontal lobe does not fully mature until between the ages of twenty and thirty***: See E. R. Sowell, P. M. Thompson, C. J. Holmes, T. L. Jernigan, and A. W. Toga's article "*In Vivo* Evidence for Post-Adolescent Brain Maturation in Frontal and Striatal Regions" in *Nature Neuroscience* 2 (1999): 859–861.

[p. 138] ***Twentysomething brains ought to afford them special services***: See "What Is It About 20-Somethings?" by Robin Marantz Henig for the *New York Times,* August 18, 2010.

[p. 138] ***Phineas Gage benefited from a sort of "social recovery"***: See Malcolm Macmillan, "Phineas Gage—Unravelling the Myth."

[p. 140] ***Researchers at the National Institute of Mental Health***: For an excellent overview of the still-developing teen and twentysomething brain, read D. R. Weinberger, B. Elvevåg, and J. N. Giedd's summary "The Adolescent Brain: A Work in Progress" for the National Campaign to Prevent Teen Pregnancy (June 2005).

[p. 140] ***Thousands of new connections that sprout do so in the frontal lobe***: For an overview of the brain changes in this last critical period, see S.-J. Blakemore and S. Choudhury's article "Development of the adolescent brain: implications for executive function and social cognition" in *Journal of Child Psychology and Psychiatry* 47 (2006): 296–312.

[p. 141] ***Larger social networks change our brains for the better***: See J. Sallet, R. Mars, M. Noonan, J. Andersson, J. O'Reilly, S. Jbabdi, P. Croxson, M. Jenkinson, K. Miller, and M. Rushworth, "Social Network Size Affects Neural Circuits in Macaques,"

Science 334 (2011): 697–700, and R. Kanai, B. Bahrami, R. Roylance, and G. Rees, "Online Social Network Size is Reflected in Human Brain Structure," *Proceedings of the Royal Society B: Biological Sciences*, published online Oct. 12, 2011.

[p. 141] ***"Neurons that fire together, wire together"***: This is Hebb's rule. It describes the mechanism of plasticity and associative learning and was postulated by Donald O. Hebb.

[p. 141] ***A time of "great risk and great opportunity"***: See any research by J. Giedd on the adolescent brain, for example his article "The Teen Brain—Insights from Neuroimaging" in *Journal of Adolescent Health* 42 (2008): 335–343. This quote is from page 341.

[p. 141] ***Frontal lobe connections we use are preserved and quickened***: Via myelination, the process by which neural axons become wrapped in a fatty sheath. This increases the speed of communication between neurons. The frontal lobe is the last part of the brain to myelinate, probably because it is the last to fully mature. Myelination ensures that the connections left after pruning will become faster and more efficient.

Calm Yourself

[p. 148] ***The brain has a built-in novelty detector***: See "Learning by Surprise" by Daniela Finker and Harmut Schotze in *Scientific American*, December 17, 2008: http://www.scientificamerican.com/article.cfm?id=learning-by-surprise.

[p. 148] ***More likely to remember the bizarre***: See P. Michelon, A. Z. Snyder, R. L. Buckner, M. McAvoy, and J. M. Zacks's article "Neural Correlates of Incongruous Visual Information: An Event-Related fMRI Study" in *NeuroImage* 19 (2003): 1612–1626, as well as

J. M. Talarico and D. C. Rubin's chapter "Flashbulb Memories Result from Ordinary Memory Processes and Extraordinary Event Characteristics" in *Flashbulb Memories: New Issues and New Perspectives,* edited by O. Luminet and A. Curci (New York: Psychology Press, 2009).

[p. 148] ***Better recall for the slides that immediately follow the snake***: See N. Kock, R. Chatelain-Jardon, and Jesus Carmona's article "Surprise and Human Evolution: How a Snake Screen Enhanced Knowledge Transfer Through a Web Interface" in *Evolutionary Psychology and Information Systems Research* 24 (2010): 103–118.

[p. 148] ***People are more likely to remember highly emotional events***: See R. Fivush, J. G. Bohanek, K. Martin, and J. M. Sales's chapter "Emotional Memory and Memory for Emotions" in *Flashbulb Memories: New Issues and New Perspectives,* edited by O. Luminet and A. Curci (New York: Psychology Press, 2009).

[p. 149] ***Twentysomethings take these difficult moments particularly hard***: See S. T. Charles and L. L. Carstensen's article "Unpleasant Situations Elicit Different Emotional Responses in Younger and Older Adults" in *Psychology and Aging* 23 (2008): 495–504, as well as F. Blanchard-Fields's "Everyday Problem Solving and Emotion: An Adult Developmental Perspective" in *Current Directions in Psychological Science* 16 (2007): 26–31.

[p. 149] ***Twentysomething brains simply react more strongly to negative***: See M. Mather, T. Canli, T. English, S. Whitfield, P. Wais, K. Ochsner, J.D.E. Gabrieli, and L. L. Carstensen's article "Amygdala Responses to Emotionally Valenced Stimuli in Older and Younger Adults" in *Psychological Science* 15 (2004): 259–263.

[p. 150] ***Positivity effect***: See M. Mather and L. L. Carstensen's article "Aging and Motivated Cognition:

The Positivity Effect in Attention and Memory" in *Trends in Cognitive Science* 9 (2005): 496–502.

[p. 152] ***Danielle's worries kept her from feeling surprised***: See S. J. Llera and M. G. Newman's paper "Effects of Worry on Physiological and Subjective Reactivity to Emotional Stimuli in Generalized Anxiety Disorder and Nonanxious Control Participants" in *Emotion* 10 (2010): 640–650.

[p. 154] ***Reevaluate situations based on the facts***: For a useful overview of emotion regulation, see K. N. Ochsner and J. J. Gross's article "Thinking Makes It So: A Social Cognitive Neuroscience Approach to Emotion Regulation" in R. F. Baumeister and K. D. Vohs (Eds.), *Handbook of Self-Regulation: Research, Theory, and Applications* (New York: Guilford Press, 2004), 229–255. And for a useful comparison of the regulatory strategies of reappraisal and suppression, see J. J. Gross and O. P. John's paper "Individual Differences in Two Emotion Regulation Processes: Implications for Affect, Relationships, and Well-Being" in *Journal of Personality and Social Psychology* 85 (2003): 348–362, as well as O. P. John and J. J. Gross's chapter "Individual Differences in Emotion Regulation" in J. J. Gross (Ed.), *Handbook of Emotion Regulation* (New York: Guilford Press, 2007), 351–372.

Outside In

[p. 157] ***Mindset***: To learn more about the growth mindset versus the fixed mindset, see any work by Carol Dweck, especially her book *Mindset: The New Psychology of Success* (New York: Random House, 2006).

[p. 158] ***In a longitudinal study of college students*** and
[p. 159] ***Individuals strongly hold either a fixed mind-***

set or a growth one: See R. W. Robins and J. L. Pals's paper "Implicit Self-Theories in the Academic Domain: Implications for Goal Orientation, Attributions, Affect, and Self-Esteem Change" in *Self & Identity* 1 (2002): 313–336.

[p. 159] ***Real confidence comes from mastery experiences***: For an overview of self-efficacy, see the definitive work by Albert Bandura, *Self-Efficacy: The Exercise of Control* (New York: Worth Publishers, 1997).

[p. 161] ***The work of K. Anders Ericsson***: The work of K. Anders Ericsson has been written about many times. For a scholarly article, see K. A. Ericsson, R. T. Krampe, and C. Tesch-Romer's article "The Role of Deliberate Practice in the Acquisition of Expert Performance" in *Psychological Review* 100 (1993): 363–406. For a more popular accounting, see chapter 2 of Malcolm Gladwell's *Outliers* (New York: Little, Brown, 2008), titled "The 10,000 Hour Rule." Also see "A Star Is Made" by Stephen J. Dubner and Steven D. Levitt in the *New York Times,* May 7, 2006.

[p. 163] ***Positive feedback would give her the opportunity to feel better***: See S. Chowdhury, M. Endres, and T. W. Lanis's paper "Preparing Students for Success in Team Work Environments: The Importance of Building Confidence" in *Journal of Managerial Issues* XIV (2002): 346–359.

Getting Along and Getting Ahead

[p. 165] ***A spirited debate among personality researchers***: For a thorough overview of the debate about personality change after age thirty, see the featured article by B. W. Roberts, K. E. Walton, and W. Viechtbauer, "Patterns of Mean-Level Change in Personality Traits Across the Life Course: A Meta-Analysis of Longitudinal Studies" in *Psychological Bulletin* 132 (2006): 1–25, the comment by P. T. Costa and R. R. McCrae in the same journal on pages 26–28, as well as the reply to the comment by the authors on pages 29–32.

[p. 165] ***Personality traits appear to be fixed after age thirty***: See P. T. Costa, R. R. McCrae, and I. C. Siegler's paper "Continuity and Change Over the Adult Life Cycle: Personality and Personality Disorders" in C. R. Cloninger (Ed.), *Personality and Psychopathology* (Arlington, VA: American Psychiatric Press, 1999), page 130.

[p. 166] ***The other side is more optimistic***: See page 14 in B. W. Roberts, K. E. Walton, and W. Viechtbauer, "Patterns of Mean-Level Change in Personality Traits across the Life Course: A Meta-Analysis of Longitudinal Studies" in *Psychological Bulletin* 132 (2006).

[p. 169] ***Employed twentysomethings are happier***: See "How Young People View Their Lives, Futures, and Politics: A Portrait of 'Generation Next' by Pew Research Center," released on January 9, 2007, at http://people-press.org/report/300/a-portrait-of-generation-next.

[p. 170] ***Life starts to feel better across the twentysomething years***: See B. W. Roberts and D. Mroczek's paper "Personality Trait Change in Adulthood" in *Current Directions in Psychological Science* 17 (2008): 31–35.

[p. 170] ***"Getting along and getting ahead"***: For articles that address social investment theory, or the idea that making commitments to social roles is how life feels better for twentysomethings, see B. W. Roberts, D. Wood, and J. L. Smith's paper "Evaluating Five

Factor Theory and Social Investment Perspectives on Personality Trait Development" in *Journal of Personality* 39 (2008): 166–184; J. Lodi-Smith and B. W. Roberts's paper "Social Investment and Personality: A Meta-Analysis of the Relationship of Personality Traits to Investment in Work, Family, Religion, and Volunteerism" in *Personality and Social Psychology Review* 11 (2007): 68–86; and R. Hogan and B. W. Roberts's article "A Socioanalytic Model of Maturity" in *Journal of Career Assessment* 12 (2004): 207–217.

[p. 171] ***Twentysomethings who don't feel they are getting along or getting ahead...feel stressed and angry and alienated***: See B. W. Roberts, A. Caspi, and T. E. Moffitt's article "Work Experiences and Personality Development in Young Adulthood" in *Journal of Personality and Social Psychology* 84 (2003): 582–593.

[p. 171] ***Even simply having goals can make us happier***: See B. W. Roberts, M. O'Donnell, and R. W. Robins's paper "Goal and Personality Trait Development in Emerging Adulthood" in *Journal of Personality and Social Psychology* 87 (2004): 541–550.

[p. 171] ***Goal-setting...led to greater purpose, mastery, agency, and well-being in the thirties***: See P. L. Hill, J. J. Jackson, B. W. Roberts, D. K. Lapsley, and J. W. Brandenberger's paper "Change You Can Believe In: Changes in Goal Setting During Emerging and Young Adulthood Predict Later Adult Well-Being" in *Social Psychology and Personality Science* 2 (2011): 123–131.

[p. 171] ***Goals have been called building blocks***: See A. M. Freund and M. Riediger's article "Goals as Building Blocks of Personality in Adulthood" in D. K. Mroczek and T. D. Little (Eds.), *Handbook of Personality Development* (Mahwah, NJ: Erlbaum, 2006), 353–372.

[p. 171] ***Stable relationships help twentysomethings feel more secure and responsible***: See J. Lehnart, F. J. Neyer, and J. Eccles's article "Long-Term Effects of Social Investment: The Case of Partnering in Young Adulthood" in *Journal of Personality* 78 (2010): 639–670; F. J. Neyer and J. Lehnart's article "Relationships Matter in Personality Development: Evidence From an 8-Year Longitudinal Study Across Young Adulthood" in *Journal of Personality* 75 (2007): 535–568; B. W. Roberts, K. E. Walton, and W. Viechtbauer, "Patterns of Mean-Level Change in Personality Traits Across the Life Course"; and F. J. Neyer and J. B. Asendorpf's paper "Personality-Relationship Transaction in Young Adulthood, *Journal of Personality and Social Psychology* 81 (2001): 1190–1204.

[p. 172] ***Relationships . . . a more mature safe haven than what we have with our parents*** and ***staying single across the twenties does not typically feel good***: See J. Lehnart, F. J. Neyer, and J. Eccles, "Long-Term Effects of Social Investment," as well as F. J. Neyer and J. Lehnart, "Relationships Matter in Personality Development."

Every Body

[p. 176] ***A 2010 report by the Pew Research Center***: See "The New Demography of American Motherhood" by the Pew Research Center for an overview of how mothers are changing. For a summary or full report, go to http://pewresearch.org/pubs/1586/changing-demographic-characteristics-american-mothers.

[p. 176] ***Women outnumber men in the workplace***: For an excellent article about how women outnumber—and arguably outperform—men at school and work in the postmodern era, see Hanna Rosin's "The End of Men" in *The Atlantic*, July/August 2010.

[p. 176] ***In a different Pew survey***: See the Pew Research Center's 2010 report "Millennials: Confident. Connected. Open to Change," found at http://pewresearch.org/millennials.

[p. 177] ***Sobering statistics about having babies after the age of thirty-five***: Except where noted otherwise, the data on fertility presented in this chapter is based on conversations with Dr. William S. Evans, a specialist in reproductive medicine in Endocrinology and Metabolism at University of Virginia Medical Center. Dr. Evans was kind enough to provide a crash course in fertility by sharing data and statistics as well as his own vast experience, and by reading a draft of this chapter to ensure its accuracy.

[p. 177] ***Medicine has been called "a science of uncertainty and an art of probability"***: This is a quote from Sir William Osler.

[p. 177] ***Older sperm may be associated with neurocognitive problems***: See S. Saha, A. G. Barnett, C. Foldi, T. H. Burne, D. W. Eyles, S. L. Buka, and J. J. McGrath's article "Advanced Paternal Age Is Associated with Impaired Neurocognitive Outcomes During Infancy and Childhood" in *PLoS Medicine* 6 (2009): e1000040.

[p. 178] ***"By the time [she] was thirty-eight or forty"***: This quote comes from "For Prospective Moms, Biology and Culture Clash" by Brenda Wilson for NPR, May 8, 2008, http://www.npr.org/templates/story/story.php?storyId=90227229.

[p. 180] ***Base rates for babies born in the United States in 2007***: The actual numbers are 1,082,837 babies born to mothers aged twenty to twenty-four, 1,208,405 born to mothers aged twenty-five to twenty-nine, 962,179 born to mothers aged thirty to thirty-four, 499,916 born to mothers aged thirty-five to thirty-nine, 105,071 born to mothers aged forty to forty-four, and 7,349 born to women forty-five and older. See National Vital Statistics Reports, Volume 57, Number 12, titled "Births: Preliminary Data for 2007," available online from the CDC at http://www.cdc.gov/nchs/births.htm.

[p. 182] ***Today, one in five fortysomething women are childless***: This data comes from a Pew Research Center report titled "Childlessness Up Among All Women; Down Among Women with Advanced Degrees," released on June 25, 2010.

[p. 182] ***Being a parent is nothing to be idealized***: For a vivid account of the plight of the modern parent, read "All Joy and No Fun: Why Parents Hate Parenting," by Jennifer Senior for *New York* magazine, July 4, 2010.

[p. 183] ***About half of childless couples are* not *childless by choice***: See J. C. Abma and G. M. Martinez's article "Childlessness Among Older Women in the United States: Trends and Profiles" in *Journal of Marriage and Family* 68 (2006): 1045–1056.

[p. 184] ***Postponing marriage and children leads to more stressful lives***: See S. M. Bianchi's paper "Family Change and Time Allocation in American Families," presented at the November 2010 conference for Focus on Workplace Flexibility. The paper can be found at http://workplaceflexibility.org. Bianchi's work was also discussed in an article titled "Delayed Child Rearing, More Stressful Lives" by Steven Greenhouse for the *New York Times,* December 1, 2010.

Do the Math

[p. 188] ***Twenty-three-year-old French speleologist***: Michel Siffre's cave experiment and resulting career in chronobiology have been written about in many places. For an interesting account, see Joshua Foer's interview with Siffre, "Caveman: An Interview with Michel Siffre," published in *Cabinet* magazine, Issue 30 (2008), and found at http://www.cabinetmagazine.org/issues/30/foer.php.

[p. 189] ***Carstensen used virtual reality***: For a full description of the project by Laura Carstensen and Jeremy Bailenson titled "Connecting to the Future Self: Using Web-Based Virtual Reality to Increase Retirement Saving," see the following website: http://healthpolicy.stanford.edu/research/connecting_to_the_future_self_using_webbased_virtual_reality_to_increase_retirement_saving.

[p. 190] ***Present bias*** and ***discount the future***: For a better understanding of these concepts, see the work of Gal Zauberman, especially the paper by D. Soman, G. Ainslie, S. Frederick, X. Li, J. Lynch, P. Moreau, A. Mitchell, D. Read, A. Sawyer, Y. Trope, K. Wertenbroch, and G. Zauberman, "The Psychology of Intertemporal Discounting: Why Are Distant Events Valued Differently from Proximal Ones?" in *Marketing Letters* 16 (2005): 347–360.

[p. 191] ***"Now-or-never behaviors***: See R. D. Ravert's paper "You're Only Young Once: Things College Students Report Doing Before It's Too Late" in *Journal of Adolescent Research* 24 (2009): 376–396.

[p. 194] ***Psychological distance between now and later***: See Y. Trope, N. Liberman, and C. Wakslak's article "Construal Levels and Psychological Distance: Effects on Representation, Prediction, Evaluation, and Behavior" in *Journal of Consumer Psychology* 17 (2007): 83–95.

[p. 198] ***"I always begin with the last sentence"***: Quote from John Irving's author website: www.john-irving.com.

Epilogue
Will Things Work Out for Me?

[p. 199] ***Mountains don't care***: A copy of this poster can be found at www.rockymountainrescue.org.

ACKNOWLEDGMENTS

"Don't write a book unless you can't *not* write it," a colleague warned. As weighty as it can be to talk about other people's experiences, I simply couldn't *not* try to tell these stories, the stories of the women and men who have shared with me the most difficult and defining moments of their lives. Years of working with twentysomethings and thirtysomethings and fortysomethings has left me with information—and opinions—I could not keep to myself. My clients and students didn't just make this book possible. They made not writing it impossible. This book is for them.

I also extend my appreciation to colleagues who helped with the book either directly or indirectly, some reading chapters or whole drafts, others providing a quotable remark, a useful reference, a respected opinion, or valued mentoring: Jennifer Ackerman, Cameron Anderson, Jessica Barnes, Leslie Bell, Natalie Boero, Charles Boisky, Jane Easton Brashares, Allison Briscoe, Diane Burrowes, Laura Carstensen, Leonard Carter, Laurie Case, Nancy Chodorow, Kathleen Davies, Daphne DeMarneffe, Rachel Ebling,

William Evans, Krista Gattis, Gian Gonzaga, Ravenna Helson, Tom Jenks, Oliver John, Emily Lape, Pema Lin, Janet Malley, Carol Manning, CJ Pascoe, Maryfrances Porter, Victoria Pouncey, Ellen Rambo, Deborah Raphael, Mark Regnerus, Richard Robbins, Brent Roberts, Molly Schnure, Bruce Smith, Abigail Stewart, Anderson Thomson, Raphael Triana, Eric Turkheimer, Jeremy Uecker, Bradford Wilcox, and Gail Winston.

I would like to acknowledge the institutions that have supported my training, teaching, research, and clinical work: Counseling and Psychological Services, Curry School of Education, and Department of Psychology at the University of Virginia; Department of Psychology, Institute of Personality and Social Psychology, Gender and Women's Studies, and Mills Longitudinal Study at the University of California, Berkeley; Access Institute in San Francisco, California; the American Psychoanalytic Association; and the National Institute of Mental Health.

From Twelve, I owe my deepest gratitude to Jonathan Karp for sharing my vision of starting a new conversation with, and about, twentysomethings. He kindly encouraged me to tell interesting stories and to have the courage of my convictions with charm; I may not have always succeeded, but it was good advice. Susan Lehman read this manuscript and offered insight that organized and sharpened these pages. I thank her for that, and for her continuing support. Cary Goldstein edited the final version of the manuscript and valiantly brought it to print. His perspective gave new life to the book and forged its final form. I also much appreciate the careful work done by copy editor Rachelle Mandik and production editor Siri Silleck.

Three twentysomethings at Twelve deserve recognition: Amanda Lang and Libby Burton read chapters and provided helpful feedback, all while handling the details that go into making a book real. Sonya Safro read the manuscript many times, keenly spotting moments when twentysomethings might turn away from me or passages where it seemed I had turned away from them. The publishing industry seems full of twentysomethings who are leading intentional lives.

Words cannot express the admiration I have for the indefatigable Tina Bennett. All I can do is thank her for being a wise agent, a discerning thinker, a crack editor, a class act, and a truly good person. Pivotal moments may be less frequent in one's forties than in one's twenties, but perhaps no one is better than Tina at making these happen at any age.

Most of all, I thank my family for giving my life meaning and perspective I did not fathom as a twentysomething. I thank my husband for enduring innumerable conversations about the book and for saying yes to anything that furthered this project, including letting me tell the pizza story. I thank my children for their patience as they waited outside my office while I wrote. Even more, I thank them for the times they just couldn't wait, when they would come bursting in through the door.

The best part about getting older *is* knowing how your life worked out.

ABOUT THE AUTHOR

Meg Jay, PhD, is a clinical psychologist, who specializes in adult development and twentysomethings, in particular. She is an assistant clinical professor at the University of Virginia, and maintains a private practice in Charlottesville, Virginia. Dr. Jay earned a doctorate in clinical psychology, and in gender studies, from the University of California, Berkeley.

ABOUT TWELVE

TWELVE was established in August 2005 with the objective of publishing no more than twelve books each year. We strive to publish the singular book, by authors who have a unique perspective and compelling authority. Works that explain our culture; that illuminate, inspire, provoke, and entertain. We seek to establish communities of conversation surrounding our books. Talented authors deserve attention not only from publishers, but from readers as well. To sell the book is only the beginning of our mission. To build avid audiences of readers who are enriched by these works—that is our ultimate purpose.

For more information about forthcoming TWELVE books, please go to www.twelvebooks.com.